London Shadows

George Godwin

Illustrated by John Brown

DODO PRESS

LONDON SHADOWS

A GLANCE AT THE "HOMES" OF THE THOUSANDS

BY GEORGE GODWIN, F.R.S.

EDITOR OF "THE BUILDER," ETC.

WITH NUMEROUS ILLUSTRATIONS BY JOHN BROWN

1854

"Not to know at large of things remote,
From use, obscure and subtle, but to know
That which before us lies in daily life,
Is the prime wisdom : what is more is fume,
Or emptiness, or fond impertinence,
And renders us in things that most concern,
Unpractised, unprepared, and still to seek."
MILTON

TO HIS ROYAL HIGHNESS PRINCE ALBERT, F.R.S.,

CHIEF COMMISSIONER FOR THE GREAT EXHIBITION OF 1851,
ETC.,ETC.

THE FOLLOWING PAGES ARE INSCRIBED

IN RESPECTFUL TESTIMONY OF CONTINUOUS EFFORTS
MADE BY

HIS ROYAL HIGHNESS

TO IMPROVE THE DWELLINGS OF THE POOR

AND

TO ADVANCE THE ARTS WHICH REFINE AND ELEVATE.

A Clerkenwell Interior

PROLOGUE.

THE war of nations is a frightful evil (great the sin of those who render it necessary), but we must not shut our eyes to the direful operations of relentless foes at home, more costly and more deadly, though carried on with fewer trumpets. The miserable condition in which thousands of human beings are condemned to pass their lives in London and other large towns is a giant evil, a giant which should be slain if we would not have it slay us. And a war against this, fortunately, is a war which can be prosecuted without fear of loss, and with the certainty of success. There is no question about this,-no doubt. To whatever extent the endeavour is made, to that extent will advantages follow; as certainly as that two and two make four, and that we are all bound by the solemnest of injunctions to bear our part in the fight, - a fight against dirt, disease, disorder, degradation, and death; - a fight in a Holy War.

Only those who have examined into the evil for themselves can judge of its enormous extent and its frightful results. We are all interested in the removal of it, immediately and personally; and yet, blinded by ignorance or trusting to chance, we shut our eyes to the fact, and go on building gaols and forming penal settlements, to punish what might have been prevented; taxing our means to pay the cost of illness and death wickedly produced, and dying ourselves, it may be said without irreverence, long before there is any real necessity for doing so.

Part of the following statements with reference to the condition of London appeared originally in "THE BUILDER," and obtained the commendation of some whose good opinion is a reward. It has been urged that the further publication of them in a cheap form might be useful, and, believing it to be of the greatest importance that the extent of the disease should be widely known, in order to induce corresponding efforts for its cure, the suggestion has been adopted. In some few instances ameliorations may have been attempted since these remarks were written; but nothing has been done to any extent. I have visited places during the last fortnight not fit for dogs, and yet which hold in every room two or three families, - holes, ill-drained, ill-ventilated, and altogether unsuited for use. In the occupants of such places-men and women with bodies to suffer and souls to be lost-the feelings are blunted, the moral perceptions distorted; decency is out of the question, and degradation nearly certain. Goodness and virtue are sometimes to be found there, wonderful to say, but the majority have no hope; progress is impossible, the future a blank: in the dirt they are, and in the dirt they must remain. A remedy may be afforded at all events we may deal successfully with the next generation, and surely, surely this should be attempted. What is hereafter set forth has not been written to make a case, but to state plain facts. The examination has been painful and disheartening : still, to succeed to any extent in obtaining for the suffering thousands dwelling-places worthy the name of HOME, where the virtues and kindly feelings *might* be cultivated, and the household gods worthily set up, would be a reward so rich that the labour of the endeavour is not to be considered. Most earnestly then, and with deep feeling, I venture to implore the co-operation to this end of all who would advance society, lessen suffering, promote the happiness of their fellow creatures, and save the frightful amount of money, power, and life, now annually wasted in this kingdom. We may all do something, and moreover we are bound to do it

"This world is full of beauty as other worlds above,
And if we did our duty, it might be full of love."

G.G.

Brompton.

CHAPTER I.

"When every man is his own end, all things will come to a bad end."

COLERIDGE.

DEEP are the "Mysteries of London," and so environed by difficulties, that few can penetrate them. The condition of large sections of its inhabitants is wholly unknown to the majority of those above them in the social pyramid, the wide base of which is made up of poverty, ignorance, degradation, crime, and misery. Much has been written on it within the last few years, and a large amount of good has been done. Still the great bulk of the people are ignorant and apathetic on the subject, blind to the extent to which they are themselves concerned in it: and, viewing the evil as a mighty one, and strongly impressed by the helpless - almost hopeless - condition of many thousands of fellow-creatures, who cannot make themselves heard unless the press speak for them, we propose entering into some particulars respecting the lodging-houses and other dwellings in London inhabited by the poorer classes, with the view of inducing efforts for their amelioration. It is quite possible to house the poorer classes comfortably and healthfully at as little cost to themselves as they now pay, and at infinitely less cost to the community at large; and what we desire is, to aid in bringing this about. As the writer has said elsewhere again and again, and the sentence has been echoed and reechoed far and wide, - homes are the manufactories of men, - *as* the home, *so* what it sends forth.

To investigate the condition of the houses of the very poor in this great metropolis is a task of no small danger and difficulty : it is necessary to brave the risks of fever and other injuries to health, and the contact of men and women often as lawless as the Arab or the Kaffir: in addition to these obstacles, there is amongst the very poor a strong feeling against intrusion few persons venture into these haunts besides the regular inhabitants, the London missionaries, the parish surgeon, and the police, and thus the extent of this great evil is imperfectly understood. A few years ago it was a fashion to visit the "Rookery" of St. Giles's, and wonder at the peculiarities of that strange land (and it was, perhaps, partly owing to these visits that some improvements were carried into effect); yet few of those visitors, and not many others, are aware of the numerous places in London and the Borough which exist at the present day in as bad a condition as any part of St. Giles's in its worst time. These blots on London abound in Whitechapel, Westminster, Spitalfields, Camden-town, Somers-town, Clerkenwell, Islington, Bermondsey, various parts of the Borough, &c. &c. In many instances these hotbeds of fever and vice are so effectually hidden by goodly houses that the inhabitants of the latter are scarcely aware of the poverty and disease which exist within a stone's throw from their own doors. These densely-peopled clumps of houses, or "Rookeries" as they are called, are mostly inhabited by the poorest Irish lodging-house keepers, tramps, coster-mongers, thieves, and the lowest class of street-walkers. In addition to these there are small shopkeepers, receivers of stolen goods, brokers, and publicans.

Of the condition of the greater part of these people it is difficult to convey anything like a just idea. It is a certain and melancholy fact that this dangerous, and to the State, expensive class of persons is alarmingly increasing in London and other large towns; and this is easily to be accounted for. Many of the poor Irish who flock to these places are either unable to get employment, or are careless in looking for it. The women and children either beg, sweep crossings, or exist (for it is nothing better) on the profits of the sale of such trifling articles as they can procure. The parents are mostly ignorant, so are the children few are sent to school: few are taught any trade; and the great majority, from an early age, gain a precarious living in the streets : many become thieves (little wonder), and in their turn teach others. Most of this class either marry young or form connections by which the numbers rapidly increase. There are other causes, which it is not our purpose in the present paper to inquire into.

It is, however, certain that one important and leading cause of this degradation is the condition of the dwellings in which thousands of these outcasts are born, and in which they live and die. Improving

2

these would do much towards improving them. Let us then penetrate some of the London shadows, and show their distressing depth, - their degrading results. When the nature and extent of an evil are thoroughly known, efficient remedies become more probable. The Act for Improving the Condition of the Common Lodging Houses seems to be working well ; but in justice to the poor, it must be followed by other measures.

So numerous are the London "Rookeries," and so generally bad, that it is difficult to fix upon a starting-point. Circumstances, however, lead us to the outwardly respectable neighbourhood of the Marlborough-street Police Court : here, close to Berwick-street, exists a little-known but badly-built and badly-inhabited collection of houses. The people of this district were, and still are, the constant plagues of the police some of the public-houses are of the worst description. Read the following printed announcement copied verbatim from the window of a chemist's shop close by: it will help to give an idea of the inhabitants:-

"LADIES AND GENTLEMEN
ARE RESPECTFULLY INFORMED THAT
BLACK EYES
ARE EFFECTUALLY CONCEALED
ON MODERATE TERMS.
*It is warranted that the Preparation is not
Injurious to the Skin.*

This chemical and artistic process should be profitable practice, provided the parties care sufficiently about disguise, for black eyes are plentiful enough. So great a nuisance and expense had this "Rookery" become to the parish and police authorities, that it was determined amongst several influential occupants in the parish to provide funds by voluntary subscription for the purchase of a large group of wretched buildings, and for the purpose of erecting on their site wholesome and convenient dwellings for the poor. A certain amount was obtained, a large square patch of the worst houses in the neighbourhood cleared away, and the new building commenced. The promoters rightly felt that the dwellings of the poor should not be demolished without providing other places which, under good regulations, they could occupy at moderate cost. Recently it was found necessary to transfer the responsibility to the Metropolitan Association for Improving the Dwellings of the Industrious Classes, of which, hereafter.

The houses destroyed were abominable, and the inhabitants most difficult material to deal with. Several very desperate characters had lived there, and only those who had seen the houses previously can form a just estimate of the benefit of their removal.

The four sides of the square in which the improvement to which we have alluded is going forward, consist of houses chiefly let in single rooms, which, before the Lodging-house Act came into operation, were occupied by numerous lodgers, male and female. The houses are mostly dilapidated and dirty in the extreme. In one of these houses, in a cellar reached by a dark staircase, the steps shaky and the stair- rails rotten, we found a dark apartment, in which were two bedsteads, with scanty and dirty covering. The flagged floor was bare and damp; in one part of the room stood a tin apparatus used for the sale of baked potatoes; partly under the beds were onions and baskets of potatoes (most of the London costermongers store their unsold fruits, flowers, vegetables, fish, and other commodities, in similar places). There was no furniture except the two bedsteads, in one of which was an Irishman, who roused up at our entrance. "Not up yet; why, it is nearly eleven o'clock!" "Is it really so late?" said the tenant of this gloomy abode ; "but then I was not home until past three this morning: I had not sold my potatoes." This man had six children and a lodger who all slept in this place, as he said ; and if it could be managed without the knowledge of the police, it is probable that several other lodgers would take up their nightly abode in it.

At the back of most of the houses alluded to, after passing through a long passage, are small, square, badly-paved courts, like that shown in the engraving (Fig. 1).

Fig.1 - Court near Berwick-street.

The water stands here and there in deep puddles. In the courts we saw were conveniences, as shown in the engraving; a dust-heap (A), formed by a large stone slab, well filled with dust and refuse. "The dust," said a person living there, "is not often taken away." At (C) is a water-tank. These are all shared amongst the lodgers in the cellars, say eight persons. If only five persons occupy each of the eight rooms in front, and six the two rooms in the back court, this is all the accommodation of water, &c., provided for fifty-four persons

On ascending the wooden steps shown in the engraving, we find the room which we have engraved (Fig. 2). We have not selected this as a harrowing example of London dwellings, although it is had enough. The court is enclosed back and front by tall houses. The room is little more than 7 feet long by 6 feet wide; the greatest height 6 feet 9 inches. The narrow bedstead, which is doubled up in the daytime, reaches, when let down, close to the fire-place. The roof and part of the walls are green and mildewed with damp : through parts of the roof the sky is distinctly visible. Our engraving makes the room appear too large.

Fig. 2. - Interior of House in Court

It may be useful to note, where practicable, the class of persons who occupy the various places visited. The room engraved is occupied by a married couple of about twenty-two or twenty-three years of age, and a little girl about two years old. The young man had been brought up amongst poor persons in the neighbourhood: his education had been neglected, but he had been employed in various ways until he obtained a situation as light porter. He married a respectable young woman, a servant. A short time after marriage he lost his situation, and failed to obtain another. By some means he and his wife *got* into the method of cutting thin wooden splints, which are used in public-houses and cigar-shops. This, he says, is "poor work : the price has become so much reduced, we are glad if we can manage to get two meals a day, and then but poor ones. We seldom can afford to get a fire except on Sunday, and perhaps on part of Monday; and this place is very cold, there are so many holes. I have spoken repeatedly to the landlord, but he has done nothing. I pay 1s. 6d. a week. I am 6s. 6d. back in my rent. The rain during the last wet weather poured into the room, sometimes upon the bed. In the morning and during the wet days, we have a pool of water under the bed and on the floor. No one lives below; it is a kind of stable, and very dirty. The little child is often ill. I have parted with many of my things." The child was small, drooping, and bleached, like many of the plants which attempt to vegetate in such places. Yet this is not an example of the direst stage of London poverty. It is but a step in the story. Here are fire-irons, and various matters which would bring a price: there the neat hand of woman - the world's blessing, and who in her lowest degradation has a perception of the beautiful, - has given a dash of taste to the arrangement. Above the fire-place are several little framed prints; one representing two lovers walking on a terrace, overlooking trees and gardens bright in the light of the clear sky: another shows a richly-furnished chamber, with a couple of more mature years : there are also some unframed prints of the young royal family, and a row of small beads are festooned in the centre. On the mantelpiece are various little baskets, and other nicknacks of no great value, but evidently relics of a more prosperous time; a little key, perhaps of some prized workbox. The cupboard without a door contains an odd collection of crockery; a candlestick, with the extinguisher on the last snuff; no food visible, except a small crust on the shelf beside the teapot. Poor as this place is, it is *still a home;* and there are several thousands of these struggling homes in London. It is painful to think what may be the next stage of this young couple's poverty. The husband may, perhaps, not get another situation as porter, or anything more profitable than the employment in which he is at present engaged.

His family will probably increase. The various illnesses of his wife, and perhaps children, will cause his little property to be periodically parted with. The landlord will see when there is barely enough left to pay arrears of rent, and the cost of bringing an execution. The goods will be seized, and conveyed away to a neighbouring broker, and then the still young couple and children are thrown houseless upon the world. The next refuge is the 1odging-house, with all its horrors, vices, and temptations. We will not at present follow them.

Let us now seek another neighbourhood. Our readers have, doubtless, heard of Agar-town and district, near King's-cross railway station I This extensive and ill-built district ranges from the railway station, past the graveyards of St. Pancras and St. Giles's-in-the-fields, and continues in a northward direction until the extremity almost forms a line of intersection with Pratt-street, Camden-town.

The Agar-town estate is built on land leased from the dean and chapter of St. Paul's; and the mode of granting leases of church lands is not calculated to ensure improvement in building, good drainage, or other measures necessary for health. This large tract of land was granted on lease to a gentleman connected with the law, Mr. Agar, after whom the district was named. Mr. Agar died, leaving his property to some very young children. At that time the large residence near Pratt-street was in the fields, and no houses had been built on the estate. Indeed, so retired was this place, that within the last fifteen or sixteen years nightingales have been heard near a clump of trees at a short distance from Mr. Agar's house. The land was, however, soon let out into small strips, on leases for thirty years. No systematic plan of drainage was laid out : in fact, the houses were planted down very much in the same manner as the wooden huts and tents at the gold diggings: each man suited his means or fancy in the erection of an edifice on the land which for a few years was, on certain conditions, his own: we cannot wonder, therefore, that great oddness, and economy, and ignorance were in many instances exhibited. The ditches, which had been originally used for draining the fields, were made to answer, to a certain extent, the purpose of drains in carrying away the refuse of the occupants. The ditches in summer time became stagnant, and diseases of the worst description were spread over the district. At the time of the last visitation of the cholera, most of these ditches or uncovered drains were piped and covered over, after great exertion on the part of some of the more intelligent of the inhabitants. Considering this large district at present little better than waste land, for many of the leases must soon expire, and thinking the site available for useful purposes, we will give a more particular description of it.

The sketch of "Paradise-row" (Fig. 3) shows a clump of houses which much belie their name, with part of the new railway station in the background. It is a neglected and unwholesome place, inhabited chiefly by costermongers. This row has long been the wonder of all visitors : in front of the dilapidated buildings are heaps of refuse the houses are of small dimensions, some of the doors near here are not more than five feet six inches high : and the smell of this place, particularly in hot weather, is dreadful, caused by the decay of refuse.

Fig. 3 - Paradise-row, Agar-town.

Leaving this point, we progress towards the northmost of the houses nearer the St. Pancras-road, which are occupied by costermongers, nightmen, chimney-sweeps, and other very pool people, who pay four, five, and six shillings per week for these dirty and confined dwellings, of four small rooms each. Wooden sheds are fixed for donkeys, used to draw trucks,-indeed, several of these most useful animals to costermongers occupy part of the family residence: dogs and pigeons are plentiful, and many desperate attempts are made to cultivate plants.

We now reach the gas-works, which are of great extent; the huge iron tanks contrasting with the pigmy dwellings; the smoke and escaped gas from this factory pervade, according to the direction of the wind, every part of the adjoining district. On the right hand is the coal depot of the Great Northern railway : in front of this passes the London and Birmingham canal, which runs through the Agar-town estate: about this part are "melters'" yards, a saw-mill, cinder heaps, and rows of houses such as we have spoken of, with large gardens in front of each : at the time of this visit the frost had partly dried the road, but a short time since it was soft mud for a depth of two feet. Some of the interiors of these cottages are deplorable; they have for their inhabitants in addition to mechanics, costermongers, and worse characters, decent persons of small income and in struggling circumstances. There are men, each with a family, and perhaps an income of £80 or £100 per year, who will be found to brave the dangers and inconveniences of these places rather than run the risk of taking an expensive house and letting off a portion, or of taking part of a house, where their whole affairs would be exposed to the other inhabitants, not to mention the inconveniences which the construction of houses not intended for several families occasions. Some of the houses at the northern end of Agar-town let from 7s. to 8s. per week: some small cottages in the King's-road, leading from the workhouse, consisting of four rooms, a wash-house, and garden, let for £28 per annum.

CHAPTER II.

WE would throw light on some of the black spots in the metropolis, - the manufactories of evil and sorrow, - to show the miserable condition in which parts of London are even now; and the want of proper accommodation for the poor. "Wounds cannot be cured without searching:" the disease must be known before a remedy can be applied with certainty of success. " But we have heard of all this before," some will probably say; " we have read in the publications of the Health of Towns Commission, and elsewhere, the fullest details of the manner in which the poor live crowded together in ill-ventilated rooms, and have no doubt in our own minds as to the depreciating effects, both morally and physically, which necessarily follow."

Very likely: but have these statements been attended to? Is anything being done effectually to remedy the gigantic evil involved I So long as No is the answer to this inquiry, as it must be at this time, so long will repetition and reurging be necessary. It is extraordinary how lightly the majority estimate human life and health, and how obstinately they persist in courses inimical to both. The education of the rising generation is what we must mainly look to for a real advance:-

"Ignorance is the curse of God,
Knowledge the wings wherewith we fly to heaven."

But, in the meanwhile, we of the present must do what is possible to rescue from the slough those who are sunk in it, and to increase the sum of human happiness.

The greatness of the task is not to be listened to as good grounds for folding the hands and doing nothing. The work of the minute coral worm is scarcely to be measured; but, each performing its appointed duty, the foundations of vast islands are laid by the tiny and short-lived labourers.

To be practical: let us look at the valley of the Fleet, Clerkenwell. Within the liberties of the City, in continuation of the new street from the end of Farringdon-street, this most abominable of rivers has been hidden from the sight; and the houses originally on its banks have to a great extent been swept away. It is true that a specimen of Field-lane (of which more hereafter), that famous mart for stolen handkerchiefs, still exists. There are also Plough-court, Plumtree-court, Holborn, and a few other bits within this part of the City, so inhabited as to give some notion of the houses formerly on the vacant space. Buildings have been cleared away, and those who inhabited them have been *driven to equally unfit lodgings in other districts* - a fact not to be lost sight of in considering the effects of the demolition of the dwellings of the poor without any provision for their reception elsewhere.

If there were no courts and blind alleys, there would be less immorality and physical suffering. The means of escaping from public view which they afford, generate evil habits; and, even when this is not the case, render personal efforts for improvement unlikely. We would have such cleared away, therefore; but it is at the same time necessary that other accommodation should first be provided for those who are driven out.

The visitor to the neighbourhood alluded to will notice in the cleared space a substantial wooden hoarding running up for some distance. A tall man may peep over it, and see and hear the "Fleet" rolling in an unwholesome stream. If we follow the course of this hoarding for some distance we shall see that the *river* enters and is hidden by a gloomy archway. Thank God! the visitor may exclaim, here is the end of the Fleet, and, with thankfulness and hopes that one day soon the part of the river before his eyes may in like manner be concealed, he wends comfortably on his way.

A more enterprising traveller, however, who, anxious to get an anecdote or two of the ancient stream, follows its apparent course in a northward direction, will find that the Fleet, like the river Mole, again appears at a short distance to the light of the day, and for several hundred yards through the dense population of Clerkenwell, he dives down various courts, and, by the favour of individuals, peeps out of dilapidated windows overlooking the Fleet in hopes to discover the end of its polluted course (for be it remembered this stream is the sewer for the refuse of a population of more than half a million of persons). Few men could view the blackness and hear the rolling of the Fleet, not to mention its effect on the other senses, without feeling pity for all residing near it. The explorer of the Fleet will find a street closely abutting upon it, on the east side of which are dense masses of buildings thickly populated: he will not fail to note the entrance to Frying-pan-alley; this way is exactly two feet six inches wide, and say twenty feet long: there would not be room to get a full-sized coffin out of this court without turning it on its edge. At the end of this narrow passage is a long line of squalid houses running in sharp perspective; little turnings, wherein are dust-bins and other matters, lead to similar courts and alleys,- Rose-alley, which-

"By any other name would smell as sweet,"

"Pear-tree-court, "Broad-court," &c., which sadly belie their names. The greater number of these houses are occupied by costermongers, and the various articles of traffic and animals required in the trade are lodged in the lower story. It would be difficult to give a complete notion of the dirty appearance of those courts and their inhabitants. On the opposite side of the way, after passing under an archway, we come to a special scene of wreck and neglect.

Few would suppose that these dilapidated buildings were inhabited, and that too in the midst of winter, by human beings. In some parts the glass and framing have been entirely removed, and vain attempts made to stop out the wind and snow by sacking and other matter. The basement is occupied by donkeys and dogs. In one of the rooms we found a very old Irish woman (who said she was more than fivescore years of age), crouching over a little fire; her son, a man about thirty years of age, lives with her. There was no bedstead or other furniture in the room; the ceiling was cracked and rotten, and the window destroyed. The rent of this room is is. 6d. per week. This description will answer for several other apartments; but the rooms in the house to the right, by the dense packing and sad poverty of their inmates, make the places already mentioned appear better by the contrast. In the first room, the windows of which were filled with tins, wood, rags, &c., we found a middle-aged Irishman mending the trowsers of a lad about eight years of age, whom he was going to despatch to "worruk, to get his living, God help him!" Other children, too young to handle a broom at a crossing, or even to beg, stood about. Several women, such as those often met with in the streets of London late at night, sat on the floor, near the black-looking fire, in idleness. There was an old bedstead in the room with straw upon it and some dirty rags; there was also a chair without a back, which was politely handed for our use. Here we heard long complaints of want of work; but our friend was evidently one of those who would not much distress himself in searching for it, - his six children will beg, - his wife will sell matches in the streets, - he will let part of his miserable tenement to lodgers,-and probably finish his useless and degraded existence in the workhouse, leaving behind him a large legacy of paupers, if not criminals. The room above presented a scene of still greater destitution. Our frontispiece represents it:-There was not a single piece of furniture in it; three beds were rolled up on the ground; against the walls at intervals the whole worldly property of the different lodgers was suspended; attached to many articles, and also suspended from the roof; were small bottles of "holy water." In some instances these little collections of effects consisted of a bonnet and cloak or shawl, with a basket used for the sale of fruit and flowers; in others, nothing but a very old basket and a ragged shawl. In one part of the room there was a woman sorting bones, pieces of iron, cinders, &c., which she had gathered in the street; in another part, between the two beds, were a few cinders, which had been sifted out and placed there for the purpose of supplying the fire, round which were squatted dirty and ill-clad women and children. This room and the room below it, already mentioned, lodge in the night time twenty-five persons. The houses in this court belong to a gentleman at Notting-hill, by whom they are let to a chimney-sweeper, who lives on the spot, and then sublets them as mentioned.

Continuing towards the north, there is a hilly street, formerly called Mutton-hill, now Vine-street; the centre of this street is reached by a sharp descent from each end. At the bottom of the banks, for these were formerly the green sides of the Fleet, are two walls, with a door in each, on which are painted communications from the Commissioners of Sewers. Many would pass here and imagine that these doors led to some neatly-paved yards; we have, however, removed the screen, that our readers may themselves see what is really behind it, namely, the Fleet.

At night, or rather early in the morning, we visited some of the low lodging-houses in the neighbourhood. The moon was shining gloriously over old Bartholomew's; the "Smoothfield" looked more like a lake than a "cattle-market," when we left the station with a serjeant of police to pursue the inquiry; but what we saw by its light, aided by our companion's "bull's eye," we will tell in the next chapter. Bacon says, "It is a poor centre of a man's actions, himself. It is right earth; for that only stands fast upon his own centre; whereas all things that have affinity with the heavens, move upon the centre of another which they benefit." But acting even on this centre (Bacon's inference is right, though his illustration is wrong, for the earth is but part of a whole), thinking only of ourselves we must, if we are wise, look to the health, the well-being, and the advancement of those beneath and around us, if it be but for the effect neglect of these may hare on our own health, well-being, and advancement.

Fig. 4 - The Fleet Ditch.

CHAPTER III.

It must not he supposed that we seek, by these papers on the dwellings of the London poor, to awaken sympathy in behalf of individuals, to be expressed by pecuniary assistance to them. Our object, it must be evident to all who will give it any consideration, is permanent improvement and general amelioration. We would show the great want there is of decent accommodation for the poorer classes, the miserable state in which thousands are lodged, the degrading and demoralizing effect of this upon the character; and then point to the fact that decent accommodation may be provided for them, and a fair return be obtained for the money laid out in effecting it, to say nothing of the sums that would be saved to the community by the diminution of crime, disease, and death (not confined, let it be remembered, to the locality of the originating hovels), to which such improvements would unquestionably lead.

Let us return for a moment to Clerkenwell, - "Nigh," as Garth wrote,-

> "Nigh where Fleet Ditch descends in sable streams,
> To wash his sooty Naiads in the Thames,"
> or, as Pope described it in nearly the same words,-
> "To where Fleet Ditch, with disemboguing streams,
> Rolls its large tribute of dead dogs to Thames."

It was about two in the morning when we wended our way to the valley of the Fleet, to visit some of the lodging-houses in that neighbourhood, starting from the police-station in Smithfield, where the suspended handcuffs of various sizes recall a time when these were more needed here than they are now. For many years, in early days, Smithfield was called "Ruffian's Hall;" by reason, "it was the usual place of frayes and common fighting during the time that sword and bucklers were in use." In the still night you may see, with the mind's eye, Rahere exhorting the people to aid him in building the Priory of St. Bartholomew: to this succeeds jousts and tournaments, with brave knights, fair ladies, and a vast deal of ruffianism: here Wallace was executed and Wat Tyler slain, and there, opposite to the entrance to the old church (the moon is just now touching with bright light the dog-tooth moulding in the entrance arch amidst modern houses),

"Christians have burnt each other, quite persuaded
That all the apostles would have done as they did."

A heap of rough blackened stones and ashes remain, underground, to mark the spot.

London is dead asleep at this time; there are few persons abroad excepting a few roisterers around the bright fires of the street coffee-stalls, but at short intervals we stumble on the quiet guardians of the City, and are reminded that, while all seems at rest, the spirit of the law watches and protects. It is not market morning at Smithfield, or there would be more bustle in Cheapside and other important parts of the City, which in the daytime overflow with passengers and carriages; at this time our boots ring with a hollow sound upon the pavement, and have an echo. The air seems denser as we approach the ditch, though it may be fancy; and it is now that bad airs become worse, and the human frame is less able to resist injurious influences.

As our business is not with the *élite* of society, we progress towards what remains of Field-lane. In St. John's-court, West-street, Fox and Knott-court, and other places, there are still some common lodging-houses; but these seem to be completely under the *surveillance* of the police, and in no instance that we saw were occupied by more than the number of lodgers allowed by the regulations. Some had been cleaned recently, and otherwise improved. There are many abominations, nevertheless, in Fox and Knott-court: if you need proof, open that door at the bottom of it, but shut it again quickly, and let us go.

The back parts of many of these premises are exceedingly filthy. At the end of the new street is the *City Hospice,* where several persons, male and female, are lodged in apartments separately arranged and well ventilated. A visit to this place would be interesting to those inquiring into the important subject of improving the dwellings of the poor, although we are not prepared to recommend the system pursued here. One good feature of this institution is the establishment of washing-places, &c., which can be used by any person (free) at any hour of the day. Adjoining this is the Field-lane Ragged School, under the patronage of the earl of Shaftesbury. In this place we found 163 lads and young men asleep; and a curious sight it was. The room is lighted with gas, and the floor is divided, by planks about a foot high, into compartments a little larger than the body of a man. In nearly all of these was a lodger, covered with a rug, and, judging from the loud snoring, sound asleep. Those who attend the school may sleep here without payment; and nearly all this sleeping assembly are without visible means of obtaining a living,-many of them are known thieves. At the end of Field-lane, the houses are occupied for doubtful purposes: in one we found a witch-like hag still waiting for business. What that business was we need not inquire. The house was a dilapidated and unwholesome den. In Field-lane there are several lodging-houses, which have the ground-floor fitted up as kitchens or coffee-shops: large coke fires were burning in these. On the seats, on the tables of the first we looked into, under the tables, and strewed about the floor, in some instances partly lying over each other, like eels in a dish, were men of various ages. In a back room, partly divided by a partition, was another fire with more lodgers, some of whom, at that late hour, had but just arrived, and were cooking their supper. There were thirty lodgers in these apartments, who pay 3d. each for the privilege of stopping here; for sleeping in the beds upstairs, 4d. a night is charged for each lodger. These houses have four rooms upstairs, many of them six. Allowing four persons in each room, and only four rooms in each house, we have

Sixteen lodgers, at 4d. per night (7 nights) £1 17s 4d
Thirty ditto at 3d. per ditto £2 12s 6d
[Total] £4 9s 10d
Per annum if always full £233 11s 4d.

This would be the night-work only; but most of their lodgers are the receivers and assistants of thieves, and no doubt many sleep during the day in order to be prepared for night-excursions, and by this means the profit of the lodging-house keeper is enhanced. We went into five of these houses, and found them all full, - of misery and vice.

Leaving Field-lane, and crossing Holborn into Shoe-lane, opposite the wall of St. Andrew's Churchyard, you reach the entrance to Plumtree-court, which has long been the haunt of fever: this court extends a considerable distance towards Farringdon-street, when it goes off at right angles to Holborn; the court is very narrow, and the drainage very imperfect. A sink at the bottom of this pestilent hole receives the greater part of the refuse of the place; it is often stopped, and then a pool of considerable extent is formed. Pulling the latch of the outer door of one of the houses here, and then entering the room on the left, with the assent of its occupants, we found an atmosphere so stifling that we were forced for a moment to retreat. There were two beds in the room : in one, which seemed to have heads all round it, were no fewer than nine women and children. They were stored so oddly and so thickly, that it was not an easy matter to count them even by the strong light of the policeman's lantern. In the other bed were a man and a lad, and in a small room, or closet leading from this room, three other persons were sleeping. There was little ventilation. Had there been *none,* assuming that each respiration is forty cubic inches (Menzies), the respirations twenty a minute (Hailer), and that the existence of .08ths. of carbonic acid is destructive (Liebig),* (*See First Report of Metropolitan Sanitary Commission, p.127) *the occupants of the front room must have died in eight hours!* We will not trouble our readers with the inference, nor need we give them further details of this quarter. Pondering on what we had seen, and weighing the possibility of improvement before the *infant-school* has done its work, we were glad to make our way homeward, to freer air. The morning was dawning, and Wordsworth gave us utterance for our impressions:-

"The city now doth like a garment wear
The beauty of the morning; silent, bare,
Ships, towers, domes, theatres, and temples lie
Open unto the fields, and to the sky;

All bright and glittering in the smokeless air.

**** *

Ne'er saw I, never felt, a calm so deep!
The river glideth at his own sweet will:
Dear God I the very houses seem asleep;
And all that mighty heart is lying still."

On the One-pair Floor.

Fig. 5.—On the Ground Floor.

The sun is up again, and we will look a little farther west. Let us examine what in Stow's time was the pleasant path "leading to the fields towards Highgate and Hampstead," and which is now called, as it was then, Gray's-inn-lane. The courts and lanes in this locality extending towards Clerkenwell have long enjoyed an unenviable celebrity; and certainly the condition of many of them, as well as of their inhabitants, is miserable in the extreme. It is difficult to find fresh words to describe the varied scenes of wretchedness to which this inquiry leads us. We will enter the worst of these courts, Charlotte's-buildings, which, whether viewed in the bright sunlight, in drizzling rain, in the twilight, or the dead of night, still has the same dismal, dreadful aspect. During the day, and particularly in the evening till about ten or eleven o'clock, the narrow area is filled with strange-looking and ragged figures, whose dresses and complexion harmonize with the grey mouldy and dingy-looking walls of the buildings. So wild and haggard is the scene, that few who have not had experience of these places and people would venture to the bottom of the court. There are fifteen houses in this narrow place. Let us take one at random, and look into the interior. We have, Asmodeus-like, removed the front wall from the top to the bottom, that our readers may examine without fear, and at their leisure, the extraordinary and distressing scene it presents (Fig. 5). Let us schedule its contents, beginning with the *ground-floor front*. There are no bedsteads, chairs, or tables, a few ragged clothes are drying before a little fire in the grate, above the mantel are a looking-glass about three inches high and some torn prints of the Crucifixion, &c.; in the cupboards, without doors, are pieces of broken crockery; a kind of bed in one corner, with children asleep; the floor rotten in many parts, the walls and ceiling sadly cracked. The rent is 2s. 3d. per week, which is called for every Monday, and must be paid at latest on Wednesday.

The ground-floor back presented a sad scene of distress, - the man, his wife, and some children earn a living by chopping fire-wood; the man had been ill, and not able to rise for two days. He was lying on a quantity of wood-shavings, and was partly covered with an old black and ragged blanket; his skin did not appear as if it had been washed for weeks; he was very ill, and evidently in a state of fever; his wife was almost equally dirty. "We have no wood to chop, was the expression of their ultimate distress. This room was much dilapidated, and they had suffered greatly during late severe weather, owing to the broken condition of the windows. The rent is 1s. 9d. per week : the window overlooks a back yard, the condition of which was shocking: the senses of these poor creatures have, however, beconie so deadened, that they seem only to be susceptible of cold and hunger, and the grossest impurity of the atmosphere is in no way cared for. Viewing the unwholesome state of the back yard of this house (the others are equally bad), and considering the numerous places in London where similar accumulations of filth are allowed, we cannot but wonder that before this time the necessity for the formation of a sanitary police has not been admitted.

The Attic.

Fig. 5, continued.—On the Two pair Floor.

The first-floor, both back and front, was crowded with inhabitants. The people acknowledged that fifteen persons slept in the two little rooms the previous night; the walls were cracked and dirty, and the ceiling constantly falls upon the floor while the inmates are taking their food : one woman said that a part of the cracked hearthstone from above had fallen amongst the children. Some of the people in the front room were employed in chopping firewood, which the children are sent out to sell. It is difficult, since the new police regulations respecting lodging-houses, to get a true account of the number who actually reside in these places, as the parties are afraid of the particulars getting to the ears of the authorities; they, however, confessed that fifteen grown people and children slept on this floor: the rent of the front room is 2s. 3d.; back, 1s. 9d. Continuing our way up-stairs, we found the state of the staircase and the rooms worse and worse.

In *the front room two-pair,* when our eyes had become accustomed to the Rembrandtish gloom, we found fifteen persons: some had been selling onions, &c. in the streets; some begging; one or two were seemingly bricklayers' labourers; and others had been working at the carrion heaps in the neighbourhood. It was a motley group: a characteristic Irishman was seated on the top of an iron cooking-pot engaged in conversation with one whom he called "Mr. D." at the chimney corner. They were exceedingly polite, and no gentleman in his arm-chair could have been more courteous than our friend on his iron throne. It is, unfortunately, difficult to get truth from the poor Irish, who will impose all manner of fables upon a stranger, and we did not find this case an exception. Nearly all the Irish by whom this court is occupied agree in stating that they were driven from Ireland by sheer distress, and that many fled from almost certain death at the time of the great famine. The rent of this floor is the same as that of the floor below.

The *attic,* in a state of repose, is shown in the top cut. This, if possible, exhibits greater poverty than below. The walls are full of large holes, and the light is visible through the roof. The rent of the attics is the same as of the floor below : it may seem strange that the prices of the rooms should not vary, but this uniformity is effected by the landlord removing those whose necessities are greater, or who may be a shilling or so in arrear of rent, to the upper quarters.

The first feeling after visiting this place is that of astonishment that persons should be allowed to let such dilapidated buildings to these poor people, who really pay more than a fair rent for a good house; the rooms are seldom unoccupied, and the loss trifling. The rent would be as follows:-

Four front rooms at 2s. 3d .... 9s. 0d. per week.
Four back do. at 1s. 9d. .... 7s. 0d.
[Total] 16s. 0d.
or £41. 12s. per annum.

The population of this small court is immense. If we take an average of fifteen persons in each floor of the houses visited, and this is greatly below the number, we find sixty persons are occupying one house, and nine hundred are in the court.

In the neighbourhood of this den are Bell-court, Tyndall-buildings, Baldwin's-gardens, Verulam-street, &c. Some of these are close courts, and others lead with various narrow ramifications towards Leather-lane. Fox-court, which for a long time was the habitation of the worst characters, is one of those passages with many branches and little courts, - some of which are very badly constructed. One small square place of this description, and which contains several tall houses, is entered by a very narrow covered entrance, in which, as if to stop the passage of even partially pure air, is situated the dust-heap, which we found overflowing, and in bad condition. The state of the houses not only here, but in Charlotte's-buildings, &c. bad as it is, is considered to have been wonderfully improved during the last few months. In Fox-court are several licensed lodging-houses; these have been limewashed, and in other ways cleansed; the space of the various rooms measured, and the number of lodgers fixed, corresponding to the size of each. In this place is a clump of fourteen small houses, which have been thus prepared for lodgers. The number allowed is seventy-five, and the beds are mostly occupied: this at the charge of 3d. for each lodger per night, would produce £6.

11s. 3d. per week, or £341 a year. In this place, Fox-court, the unfortunate known in literature as Richard Savage, was born of the countess of Macclesfield. In Portpool-lane is an improved building, erected under the superintendence of the Society for improving the Condition of the Working Classes-part of the funds for the erection of this building was provided by subscriptions collected in the London churches on the Thanksgiving-day for the departure of cholera. It is a great advantage to the neighbourhood, and consists of a very large washhouse, apartments for ironing, &c. It has been converted to its present purpose from the wreck of a brewhouse. Underneath the washhouse the cellars have been divided and fitted with closets to enable the costermongers to store their unsold goods, instead of taking them into rooms so thickly occupied as those we have mentioned.

Each closet is provided with a hock and key, and a small weekly sum is charged for this~ and for accommodation for their barrows, &c.; there are also two sets of rooms for families, similar to those erected by the Society in other parts of London, and rooms for single women of good character; these rooms are neatly fitted with washhand-stand, two iron bedsteads, mattresses, &c. they are plentifully supplied with water, and well ventilated: the rent of each of these rooms is 2s. per week: they are mostly occupied by two persons, who pay thus 1s. a week for a comfortable lodging, partly furnished. The great advantage of houses of this description for needlewomen and poor persons who take in washing, which they can complete at the washhouse opposite, is evident; and the good will be great if it can be shown that this class of buildings will pay a fair return on the cost of erection at this rent.

Something should be done with Charlotte's-buildings forthwith. Few of the countless throng who flood the paths in Gray's-inn-lane have any knowledge of the hot-bed of disease and vice which exists within a dozen yards from them.

CHAPTER IV.

CAPTAIN HAY'S report "on the Operation of the Common Lodging- House Act" in 1853, states that up to December, 1852, 3,300 persons keeping common lodging-houses, accommodating nearly 50,000 nightly lodgers, were under police inspection; and the number is now very much greater. The cases given serve to show over what a wide district the dreadful state of things already set forth by us extends. In a small room in Rosemary-lane, near the Tower, fourteen adults were sleeping on the floor without any partition or regard to decency; and in an apartment in Church-lane, St. Giles's, not 15 feet square, were *thirty-seven men, women, and children, all huddled together on the floor.*

As Captain Hay truly says, "The efforts of parties well inclined to promote the well-being of society will be of little avail whilst there are such causes in operation, sufficient to counteract all the exertions made to this end. Churches, schools, free libraries, and mechanics' institutes, all excellent in themselves, will be found to have but small results, whilst large masses of the population grow up so immersed in ignorance and vice as to look on it with complacency, and to live in it without disgust."

What we have ourselves seen surpasses belief, and, moreover, has features which prevent us from going into details of the worst portion. Under the pressure of professional occupations which absorbed the day, we have, during the night, under a sense of duty, penetrated some of the darkest recesses of Whitechapel and its neighbourhood, and have seen men and women under circumstances wherein virtue is impossible, and indulgence in vice or the commission of crime seems scarcely other than natural.

O you! who, early taught what is right, and, out of reach of want, are comparatively little tempted, - who are restrained as well by fear of the opinion of your class as by your knowledge and religion, - view with charity and mercy the errors of your less fortunate brethren.

Let these scenes, however, pass. We will not pain our readers with the details, but will wait for the morning, and be statistical and cool.

The eastern portion of London, comprising the districts of Bishopsgate-street, Whitechapel, Goodman's-fields, Radcliffe-highway, Wapping, Commercial-road, Mile-end, Spitalflelds, and Bethnal-green, extending over a large surface, and containing an immense population, is unknown land to many thousands. To form an idea of its continued rows of lanes and streets, let our readers refer to the map of London, and they will not fail to be struck with the size of this large portion of the metropolis, which is to a sad extent benighted and neglected. We will take a very small part of this space, viz., Bishopsgate-street and part of Whitechapel, and will commence with *New-court,* Charles-row, near Whitechapel church, - a court containing eight houses, with two rooms in each. This place has long been inhabited by low Irish, and has been the plague of the whole district. The condition of the houses is bad; and they contained, before the interference of the police, not less than 300 men, women, and children. There was only one place of convenience for 300 persons. The condition of the court at the time of our visit was shocking. The water was served, or wasted rather, half an hour each day, and this was almost the whole supply; for only a small cask was placed for the permanent reception of water. This court has lately been purchased by a neighbouring manufacturer, for the purpose of extending his premises; and by this time, the whole of the tenants may have been dispersed to other places. An Irishman, of pale and unhealthy countenance, evidently half fed, said, when he left that place he did not know where to go; he would be obliged to *"intrude upon his friends."* He had a wife and one child : two little children had died of fever. The young child was bleached, and although fifteen months old, did not look more than six or seven months. The face of the woman was disfigured by disease. A middle-aged woman, who said she had been turned out of the workhouse, was lying on the floor on a quantity of shavings. The charge for a bed of shavings amongst this class of poor people is one penny a day and night. The other inmates of this house had left, and the whole had to be turned out next morning the week's rent of the two wretched rooms in this house was 2s. 6d.: the Irishman who kept the house works at Covent-garden market,-traversing the long distance from this place to the market throughout the working days as early as four o'clock in the morning: from December till the beginning or middle of March (except Christmas week) his work is "very bad." He did not think that during the months stated his average earnings amounted to more than 2s. 6d. or 3s. a week; some days he did not even get 3d. : he had been obliged to live this distance from Covent-garden market in consequence of not being able to meet the expense of rent nearer, or rather was not able to find a place, for which he could help to pay by means of sub-letting. If obliged to obtain shelter in a lodging-house, he would be charged 3d. a night for himself, 3d. for his wife, and 1½d. for the child: this would be 7½d. a night, or 4s. 4½d. a week (much more than the man's present income.)

Serjeant Price, an officer of the metropolitan police force, who had been intrusted with the direction of the lodging-houses in this district, gave this account of the former condition of New-court :-.- House No 1. ground-floor, Haslin and his wife, - with daughters aged 17, 14, and 8; visible means of living, - by selling lucifer matches in the streets. Other floor, Flinden, his wife, a boy 17, and a girl 15, who sold onions and lucifers: the father had been out of work for three years. No. 2. John Collins paid 1s. 3d. per week for his room (ground-floor), occupied by the keeper, John Collins, his wife, boys 16 and 10, and girl 17, sleeping on the floor; no bedsteads, no bedding. Above, Bridget Horsam, a boy 10 years old, and Joanna Collins, the keeper's sister, sleeping on the floor; in all, eight persons in this house, the space of the two rooms sufficient for the accommodation of three persons, allowing 30 superficial feet for each. The house was dirty, dilapidated, and swarming with vermin: this was the condition of two houses after they had been *thinned* by the police. The following is an account of part of a house of ten rooms in this neighbourhood (Rosemary-lane) let to the poor Irish at 1s. 8d. per week: one of these rooms, kept by Daniel Jones, contained five beds, as they were called; but which, in fact, were nothing but bundles of rags, similar to those described in Clerkenwell. In "Bed" No. 1, Daniel Jones, the keeper, his wife, and children aged 8, 7, and 5 years.- "Bed" No. 2, occupied by Cornelius Toomey (paid 6d. a week to the keeper), John and Peter Shea, in the same bed, paid 6d.

each: 1s. 6d. for this bed. -"Bed" No. 3, John Sullivan and his wife, paying 7d. per week.- "Bed" No. 4, Cornelius Haggerty, his wife, boy 13, and girl 11; pays 1s. per week.- "Bed" No. 5, Patrick Kelly and wife, paying 11d. : in all, 14 persons in one room ; the original rent, 1s. 6d. The keeper received from lodgers 4s. per week. At the time of Serjeant Price's visit (24th of August, 1852) the greater portion of these persons were, in a state almost of nudity, huddled in this manner together.

Charles-row, in which is situated the court above described, is a narrow street of small houses, occupied at one end by poor Irish, and at the other by German musicians, sugar-bakers, &c., who live very thickly together.

In many streets adjoining are places over-populated and very unwholesome; indeed, Whitechapel church may be considered to be the centre of an immense mass of poverty, vice, and crime. Whitechapel is on the north and south divided by many streets and narrow courts, which are inhabited by very poor people, many of whom are weavers, Irish tailors, Jews, costermongers, dock labourers, and thieves ; the great extent of destitution is alarming.

For an hour or more we traversed narrow alleys and places which do not deserve the name of streets. Some of the courts were in decent condition; but, although in most instances the places within the liberties of the city are provided with main drains, many of them, owing to bad pavement and the dirty habits of the people, were partly strewed with decaying matter and stagnant water. In a narrow passage near "Rag-fair," there is a piece of land in a close neighbourhood, covered with the refuse of fish, vegetables, broken baskets, dead cats and dogs, piled up, enough to create a fever in any neighbourhood. Before the summer weather sets in, a remedy for such abuses should be found. In most of the small courts in this neighbourhood the landlord obtains a rent of 3s., 3s. 6d., and even 4s. for two very small rooms, and surely ought to attend to the provision of proper drainage and paving.

It seems difficult to discover the climax of London poverty and destitution. In every depth there is a deeper still. The prices of various kinds of provisions in these neighbourhoods give a forcible notion of the condition of their swarming population. In most of these neighbourhoods you can purchase a halfpenny worth of fish or a halfpenny worth of soup, and other matters in proportion. The luxuries are singular in their price and character: a farthing's worth of damaged oranges, for example, being hawked about the streets and sold in shops. "Rag-fair," that well-known mart for every description of second-hand clothing, will supply good habits at any price.

If some of our readers wish to judge for themselves, Cutler-street, a turning in Houndsditch, will lead them to the district. It is a curious scene : hundreds of people are assembled in the streets, which are so thickly covered with merchandise, that it is difficult to step along without treading on heaps of gowns, shawls, bonnets, shoes, and articles of men's attire. "Here Greek meets Greek," and not without "the tug of war." No person can form an idea of this anomalous multitude but by a visit. All poor and squalid; the children pinched and bleached, not "brought up," but, as Lamb says, "dragged up." Here may be seen in one of the markets, formed by some of the pillars and covering of the Hyde-park Exhibition, the great dealer, standing in his well-known place, and purchasing many cart- loads of clothing for exportation to the colonies, Ireland, and elsewhere; and other dealers of various grades, until we reach the merchant whose capital is less than a shilling, and who daily gets a *living* by the purchase of shoes, hats, and other matters, the uses of which, looking at their condition, it would be difficult to guess. Interesting as is this phase of London life, it would be foreign to our present purpose greatly to extend particulars : we cannot, however, avoid saying something more, our object being to show, by the provision of clothing made at "Rag-fair," the poverty of a class.* (* There is another Rag-fair of ancient date, near the Tower, - Rosemary-lane.)

One of the London missionaries (a body whose valuable services can only be properly appreciated by those who understand the nature and extent of the evil to which we are directing attention) says:-

"Persons who are accustomed to run up heavy bills at fashionable tailors' and milliners', will scarcely believe the sums for which the classes we are describing are able to purchase the same articles for their own rank in life."

A missionary who recently explored Rag-fair, reported that a man and his wife might be clothed from head to foot for from 10s. to 15s. Another missionary stated that 8s. would buy every article of clothing required by either a man or a woman, singly. In Pennant's time it was less. He says (speaking of the other Rag-fair), that the dealer pointed out a man to him, and said: "Look at him. I have clothed him for fourteen-pence. A third missionary reported : "There is as great a variety of articles in pattern, and shape, and size, as I think could be found in any draper's shop in London." The mother may go to "Rag-fair" with the whole of her family, both boys and girls,- yes, and her husband, too, and for a very few shillings deck them out from top to toe. I have no doubt that for a man and his wife, and five or six children, £1 at their disposal, judiciously laid out, would purchase them all an entire change. This may appear to some an exaggeration: but I actually overheard a conversation in which two women were trying to bargain for a child's frock; the sum asked for it was 1½d. and the sum offered was a penny, and they parted on the difference.

The following is the copy of the bill delivered by the dealer to one of the missionaries, who was requested to supply a suit of clothes for a man and woman whom he had persuaded to get married several years after the right time:-

"A full linen-fronted shirt, very elegant . . . . . 6d.
A pair of warm worsted stockings 1d
A pair of light-coloured trousers 6d
A black cloth waistcoat 3d
A pair of white cotton braces 1d
A pair of low shoes 1d
A black silk velvet stock 1d
A black beaver, fly-fronted, double-breasted paletot coat, lined with silk, a very superior article 1s. 6d

A cloth cap, bound with a figured band 1d
A pair of black cloth gloves 1d
[Total] 3s. 3d.

The man had been educated, and could speak no fewer than five languages; by profession he was, then, however, nothing but a dust-hill raker.

The bill delivered for the bride's costume was as follows

"A shift 1d
A pair of stays 2d
A flannel petticoat 4d
A black Orleans ditto 4d
A pair of white cotton stockings 1d
A very good light-coloured cotton gown 10d
A pair of single-soled slippers, with spring heels 2d
A double-dyed bonnet, including a neat cap 2d
A pair of white cotton gloves 1d
A lady's green silk paletot, lined with crimson silk, trimmed with black 10d
[Total] 3s. 1d.

The goods were selected by the missionary, and at the bottom of the bills the merchant marked:-

"P.S.-Will be very happy to supply as many as you can find at the same prices."

Petticoat-lane, not long before Strype wrote, had hedge-rows and elm-trees on both sides, "with pleasant fields to walk in." Close by, in Gravel-lane, till recently, stood the "Spanish Ambassador's house." Many of the courts and alleys leading out of Petticoat-lane now are in a miserable state. At each corner of the *lane* where it opens into Whitechapel High-street, is a public-house Many of the courts out of Bishopsgate-street are also very bad. Maitland, speaking of some of the alleys, &c., in Bishopsgate-street ward, describes them as "inconsiderable," "small and ordinary," " long and mean," "narrow and ordinary," &c.

Fig. 6. - The Dead and the Living : Bishopsgate-street District

Since the time of Maitland's survey (1735), the condition of these numerous alleys and lanes has become worse. Dtiring a visit at night of some hours' duration, we found in the interior of these dwellings varied and painful scenes of poverty. Some of the inmates of these houses are Irish tailors, who are much overcrowded, and a great plague to the magistrates and the police. Generally speaking, the people of this district, although struggling and very poor, have mostly some little stock of furniture, and a desire to preserve appearances. In Half-moon-street, which turns out of Bishopsgate-street, next the "Sir Paul Pindar," there are courts of miserable character. The houses in "Thompson's-court" are in a frightful condition, and in "Thompson's rents" they are even worse. Order, cleanliness, or decency is out of the question.

Fig. 6. represents a scene which we have met with more than once during our perambulations,-the coffin of a dead child in the midst of the sleeping living. In a single room the family sleep, work, eat, and perform the various duties of life in company with the dead, and the evil is increased by the length of time the poverty of parties obliges them to retain the corpse until what they consider proper preparations have been made for the funeral: this seldom takes place in less than a week; instances have been known of the interment having been put off for twelve days or a fortnight. This is a difficult matter to deal with, for the prejudices of the uninstructed are strong against the removal of the bodies until they are taken to the graveyard. It is most desirable that the feeling should be overcome, and proper places be provided for the reception and retention of the dead until the proper time for interment.

The contemplation of the swarms of children which fill the miserable dens we are describing is saddening in the extreme, reflecting, as one naturally does, on what their career, with very few exceptions, *must* be, and what it should and might be.

The friends of the poor child in its little coffin may rejoice!

CHAPTER V.

SOME of our readers will perhaps say to us, - "Your statements are too truthful, too minute, and they give us pain." We regret to be forced to give pain what we have seen and what we have written have caused more grief to ourselves than to our readers; but the necessity is so great, the duty, as it seems to us, so imperative, that we cannot yet either pause in our course or change it. It is time the whole truth were known it is time that "improvers" were made to feel strongly that when they knock down houses occupied by the poor in the neighbourhood of their "work," drive them forth, and do not provide other habitations for them, they must necessarily increase the evils of overcrowding already in operation, and are guilty of wrongdoing.

We do hope, too, to do something towards removing prejudices on the part of the lower classes, which stand in the way of amelioration, - the prejudice, for example, already referred to, which would lead the occupants of a single room, ill-ventilated and over-filled, to retain the body of a deceased relative amongst the living rather than deposit it in a fitting reception-place, to wait the appointed time for burial. The feeling which prompts it is a holy one: far be it from us to depreciate it, still less to scoff; but duty must overweigh feeling : the living have a stronger claim upon us than the dead.

A startling example of the practice came before us the other day, when opening a cupboard in a miserable room in the neighbourhood of Gray's-inn-lane, we found, shut up with the bread and some other matters, *the body of* a *child,* without a coffin, but decently disposed. The child had been dead a week: on one of the shelves was its little mug, marked "Mary Ann," with some broken crockery. The man's wife had died a few weeks before, and had been kept in the same room fourteen days amidst a family of children. The opponents of legislative interference in such cases should reflect on the wide injury to health committed by this permissive poisoning, to say nothing of its effect on the character of the people. We had prepared a sketch of the closet, but its aspect was so painfully repulsive that we have withheld it. Truth is often less truth-like than fiction.

Let us leave this part of our subject and walk to *Drury-lane*. Throughout a considerable portion of Drury-lane, Wych-street, Holywell-street, and even the great thoroughfare of the Strand, there was until very lately no sewer, and, consequently, the inhabitants were obliged to submit to the infliction of cesspools under many of the houses, causing (particularly in crowded courts) the greatest damage to health. In Wych-street and Holywell-street many of the houses are of considerable antiquity, and although, in some instances, inhabited by improper characters, are not so overcrowded or so neglected (except in the matter of drainage) as to require particular notice. In Newcastle-street, and the places adjoining-Drury-court and the narrow lanes leading from it-the houses are in decent condition, and by means of an association formed amongst the neighbours, have been freed from many troublesome inhabitants : the same may be said of Craven- buildings, Feathers-court, White Hart-street, and others.

Fever has been a frequent visitor to this part of Drury-lane, and the cholera of course found it out. There are many courts and lanes in Drury-lane, the rent of a single room in which varies from 1s. 9d. to 2s. and 2s. 6d. per week. Many of these houses and those surrounding them are occupied by persons who obtain their livelihood at Covent Garden market. In the direction of Covent Garden market, Crown-court, Rose-street, and other places in the vicinity are unhealthy and much neglected. From Long-acre to the main street of St. Giles's the lanes and courts are occupied by numbers of poor Irish, costermongers, foreigners, and persons of loose character, and, as might be expected, the houses are dirty in the extreme.

Near the top of Drury-lane, on the west side, are some ancient wooden houses, now occupied as cow-sheds. On the opposite side of the street, with an undertaker's shop placed most ominously at each side of the entrance, is a place called the Coal-yard. At some distance down this place, on the fight-hand side, is the following rudely-painted notice:-

Old Original
Oyster, depot
Live and Let Live.

Having passed the oyster-shed of this cosmopolitan worthy, who has expounded the above very proper sentiment, although he could not call his oysters as witnesses to prove that he follows his own teaching, we came to an archway, under which was a large collection of stable and cow-shed refuse : and having with difficulty managed to pass this miry spot, discovered a narrow place called King's Arms-yard, containing at least a dozen houses on the two sides, erected with a sort of gallery in front over stables. In this place were several cart-loads of refuse, similar to that already described. The smell and appearance of the place were shockingly bad. The daintily-dressed lady in the blue brougham now standing at the corner, scarcely guesses her proximity to so much "dirt and distress, though the nice face looks well disposed to pity and give aid, if aid were practicable. The rooms are much out of repair. For one, in which we found a man and his wife and five children (supported by the sale of flower papers), the rent is 2s. 6d. a week.

Within a stone's throw of this very spot the Great Plague of 1665 first broke out in London. It is distressing that, in spite of cautions and advice, though nearly 200 years have elapsed, this neighbourhood should still be allowed to be a harbour for fever and other epidemics. Dr. Sutherland, in his cholera report of 1848-49, writes,- "Suffice it to say that cholera, true to the laws by which epidemics are governed, followed the usual track of the fevers by which Edinburgh and Leith are scourged, locating itself in the same filthy closes, occupying the same ill-ventilated and over-crowded tenements, not unfrequently carrying off its victims from the selfsame rooms which its fatal ravages nearly depopulated in the epidemic of 1832."

Fever is rife in this neighbourhood : on the Sunday before our visit four bodies were taken from Wild's-buildings; and we heard a little girl quietly advising another child not to go into a certain passage, lest she should get the fever. Although the houses about here are dirty and ill-drained, they are in tolerably good repair. The waste of life and increase of pauperism in this neighbourhood are very considerable, to a great extent caused by the want of cleanliness and the ill arrangement of the dwellings. The correctness of this statement is shown by the contrast in the health of the lodgers in the model lodging-house for men hard by, which has been opened for six or seven years, with that of the general neighbourhood. This place was altered to its present use by the Society for Improving the Condition of the Labouring Classes; and it is gratifying to find that even in this neighbourhood the benefit of well-ventilated lodgings is properly appreciated. The house contains eighty-two beds, a large sitting- room or kitchen, accommodation for washing, a small library, &c. : the charge for lodging here is 4d. per night, or 2s. a week: many of the lodgers have resided here for some time, one so long as five years. The manager of - the place says, that there are never fewer than seventy-five lodgers each night, and that generally all the beds are occupied. When the cholera was carrying off people on all sides, there did not occur a single case here ; and scarcely any illness which required hospital care has happened in it since the opening of the building.

Fig. 7.- A Weaver's Room in Spitalfields

"From dirt comes death:" there is no mistake about it, and the oftener this assertion is repeated, and the more universally it is impressed and acted on, the better for the world.

Continuing our walk, we pass Church-lane, the remaining portion of St. Giles's Rookery; but this has been so frequently described, that it is unnecessary to enter into particulars. It is still a sad place, and is occupied by the worst characters. We would direct attention to places less known, but which in their way are equally pernicious.

When we were in the Bishopsgate district, we made an examination of the houses occupied by the weavers in Spitalfields, and gathered some information concerning them which may interest our readers. The distress here is very great, and although the houses are for the most part in better condition than some we have described, and the weavers a respectable class of persons, the close crowded rooms in which they work, with other local causes in operation, produce illness and shorten life. We give a sketch of one of the rooms we entered, where the father and mother were continuing their midnight toil amidst the sleeping children spread about the apartment (Fig. 7).

They were at work on white watered silk for wedding dresses!

In one room we found a scene which had been described by anticipation:-

"A poor worn weaver there works for his bread-
Working on, working on, far in the night;
His daughter breathes hollowly, lying a-bed,
And the wasting clay
Lets the spirit play
Over her face with a flickering light!

But the loom is stopped ; and down by the bed
The father kneels by his dying child;
But vainly he speaks - her time is sped;
No answer there comes to his outcry wild,

For the child stares out with her glazed eyes,
Till the eyes turn back-and she silently dies
And they call it a Fever,
Putrid or low;
But I and the weaver
Both of us know
That the fetid well-water, and steaming styes,
And the choked drains' gases, that unseen rise,
Subtle and still,
Sure and slow,
Certain to kill
With an unheard blow,
Are the fiends who poisoned that maiden's breath,
And cling to her still as she sleeps in death!"

Again and again we would assert, that as you lead men and women to appreciate cleanliness, light, air, order, you make them better citizens, increase their self-respect, and elevate them in the social scale. By the miserable dwellings to which thousands in this and other great towns are condemned, we are educating them *downwards*, - an easy process, with frightful results. It cannot be too often repeated, that the health and morals of the people are regulated by their dwellings.

CHAPTER VI.

THE examination we have commenced disheartens and distresses. Nothing short of personal experience would have led us to believe in the frightful amount of ignorance, misery, and degradation which exists in this wealthy and luxurious city,-this city of 300,000 houses and two millions and a quarter of persons. The number of *children* who at this time are being educated in vice, fitted for disturbing and injuring society, forbidden from good, and prepared for a life of misery,-children who have no affections or ties; in whom natural good feelings have been quenched; who have no advisers but the bad; no home, no hope ;-is perfectly appalling. They are to be counted in thousands; we fear to say how many. Can nothing be done to save them, and so save society? Here is a fertile field appealing for labourers to the Christian, the philanthropist, the political economist, and the mere egotist, who would save himself money and annoyance by preventing, instead of punishing. Let us remember there is no irremoveable reason why these children should grow to be disorderly and lawless, - liars, thieves, perhaps murderers; they were born as capable of good as your own offspring; and, with the same nurture and teaching, would make as useful members of society. Lead them into good habits; imbue them with right principles,-and their lives, in the natural course of things, will be in accordance with these habits and principles. Equally as a matter of course will the lives of these poor outcasts follow the training they are now receiving. Knowing the seed, we know what the plant must be. It seems almost an injustice to punish for a natural result.

Here, we feel satisfied, is a right spot for the spade of those who would reap a rich harvest of good, and earnestly we pray that they may be found.

The same course of argument proves irresistibly the importance of improving the dwellings of the poor, and the evil which is being done by all acts which tend to crowd men and women into unsuitable, ill-drained, ill-ventilated, and dilapidated buildings. The rapidity with which this changes the character of the occupants is startling to those who have not before observed it.

We are being led away, however, from our original intention, which was to give some additional information concerning the weavers of Spitalfields, in accordance with our promise in another chapter. This large district, inhabited by silk weavers, is but little known, except to those whose business is connected with the place; it has, however, remarkable features, and is well worthy of a visit. Some of the streets are composed of well-built houses, from three to four stories in height, having, in the upper rooms, glazed windows extending the whole length of the houses, which give them a peculiar appearance. The general aspect of the neighbourhood is cleaner, and is less squalid than in the other regions of the "East," and the inhabitants are also better clad and neater in their appearance. The weavers are mostly of French descent, their forefathers having been driven to London by religious persecution shout 150 years ago, and it is curious to note how much they have preserved the national style and peculiarities to the present day. There is an immense number of them, and they are mostly remarkable for intelligence. They suffer much privation, struggling to some extent as they do against machinery. In Spital-square, which is close to Bishopsgate-street, the master weavers live. Leading from this are streets, black and dilapidated, which are becoming more and more crowded in consequence of the removal of houses by the Eastern Counties Railway Company, who have purchased part of the neighbourhood. In other districts, owners of houses will not permit the looms to be set up. If this should aid in leading some of the weavers to seek other employment it would be fortunate their present condition is miserable, nor is there any prospect of improvement. Amongst the principal streets thus occupied, are Grey Eagle-street, Black Eagle-street, Pearl-street, Phoenix-street, and Hope-street. Seeking one of the most respectable of the class, who lives out of the web of streets in a cottage with a garden, we found the room comfortably furnished. In a cupboard in the corner, was a collection of old china and glass, which had probably been brought from abroad at the time that persecution drove his ancestors for refuge to this country; and since, even in times of difficulty, carefully preserved. This weaver, whose name was decidedly French, and who, although a very old man, was intelligent, cheerful, and gentlemanly in his manner, had two daughters, well-dressed young women, of from twenty-three to twenty-five years of age, who assisted their father in working at the loom. The mother had died during the last visitation of cholera, and both the daughters had been ill, one of them dangerously. Many of their neighbours were attacked, and several died. The mother was upwards of sixty years of age at the time of her death, and for forty-five years had been entirely employed in weaving white silk. Year after year they had found it necessary to work more hours, even then receiving a less amount of money than formerly. This had never been a large family, and the parents had been able to rear the daughters in a time of comparative prosperity to present usefulness. In many cases, however, he said, families laboured on in the midst of abject poverty and distress; and ret, notwithstanding privations and temptations, and that these weavers have at times from £20 to £40 worth of property intrusted to their care, a breach of confidence seldom happens. The old weaver said, in his youth the weavers generally had a gala day once a week, when some of the most active and vicious would amuse themselves with bull- baiting, dog-fighting, and cock-fighting, and others would enter into rivalry with their tulips and pigeons.

The Spitalfields weavers are still fond of flowers, and few houses, even of the poorest, are destitute of a bit of "greenery;" they complain that they have now short time for the healthful recreation of the garden; still, however, some of them work in it a little, and many rear pet pigeons and canaries. The Spitalfields weavers are greatly attached to their own neighbourhood, and many old men are known not to have travelled during their long lives farther than King's-cross on one side, and London-bridge on the other. Two old men we met with had never seen the Euston-square station, nor had either travelled by railway or steamboat; yet they were not destitute of intelligence, and pointed with some pride to the pattern of flowered velvet on their looms. The weavers, like the Northumbrian miners, and other class workers, almost invariably intermarry with each other. Spitalfields weavers' sons have constantly intermarried with Spitalfields weavers' daughters, and thus to the present day have preserved the peculiarities to which we have alluded.

In this district a model building was erected a few years since, by the Metropolitan Association for Improving the Dwellings of the Industrious Classes, and attached to the building is a dormitory and other accommodation for single men. It is to be regretted, that notwithstanding the goodness of the accommodation, the establishment has not been so fully occupied as is desired. Yet, considering the habits of the greater part of this population, the circumstance is not so much to be wondered at. We spoke to several young weavers and other mechanics residing in the district, and found that they all preferred a lodging where they could to a certain extent have some of the social advantages of home. They liked their tea better, they said, if they took it beside some one who would supply the place in conversation of a mother or sister.

Endeavours have been made by two of the City missionaries to give the advantages of education to the children of the weavers and others who are poor, in this neighbourhood. Although the silk weavers are shrewd and intelligent, they had seldom, until solicited, sent their children to school, the reduced wages of the weavers rendering it necessary to use the labour of the children, even when quite young, in "winding quills" (a process needed in silk weaving), in order to increase the income of the family. Schools without cost to the pupils, but at painful exertion to the missionary, are opened, we understand, early in the morning, at intervals during the day and evenings, and during Sundays, by which arrangement education is beginning to spread amongst the young, and will no doubt be the means of fitting many for other duties than that of weaving. Nothing is so much wanted for the improvement of the sanitary condition of the poor as knowledge, for they are at present-speaking of the mass-perfectly unconscious of the effects of the bad atmosphere, and other evil conditions in which they and their children exist. The following notes from the conversations of Spitalfields weavers may be interesting.

A weaver, about thirty years of age, was working flowered silk, at 8½d. a yard. He said *he worked from fourteen* to *sixteen hours a day.* "My earnings from Christmas to Christmas last year were not more than 10s. a week. I am obliged to 'play' when work is slack ;-that means, after finishing a 'cane' (an inch of silk, &c.), I have to wait until more is ready; sometimes this is a fortnight, or three weeks, or perhaps more. The slack times cause wages to be reduced. This is not done in a hurry, but by a halfpenny, or even a farthing a time. A man with a family calls at these bad times for work, and is shown some for which something less than his former price is offered : to save his family from the workhouse he agrees. I never in my experience knew the price of work again raised when once reduced. Five years ago I remember very well I could have earned with greater ease and in less time 16s. than I can now 10s." An old woman, the widow of a weaver, whose husband had died a short time since, said she earned 4d. a day by winding satin (working thirteen or fourteen hours a day); her daughter 2s. 6d. a week for working the same long horn's. The rent of their room was 1s. 6d. a week.

A weaver, his wife, and two grown-up daughters, working at ultramarine and crimson velvet, said they could each complete one yard in a day of from thirteen to fourteen hours, for which they were paid 1s. 3d. a yard: this would come to 7s. 6d. a week for each person, but there are many drawbacks. "I have a yard measure there," said the man, pointing to his loom, "exact according to Act of Parliament, but I never take home any work without having a deduction made in consequence of the difference of measure. A web of velvet is worth, when finished, about £10 10s. in the market; so on our four looms we have forty guineas' worth of property at the least. If it should happen that a web should be lost, either by roguery or accident, the whole of the weavers in the employ of the person to whom the lost web belonged would have a sum stopped from each until the amount was entirely made up," which, together with the time spent in waiting for work, would reduce the wages of this family to about 5s. a week each, - £1 in all; and in order to live comfortably and have sufficient space for their work, they are obliged to pay as rent not less than 5s. a week, leaving 15s. a week for food and clothing.

In another house, a weaver was waiting for work; his wife was weaving black silk scarfs for gentlemen. This woman was weaving silk which took sixty-four threads to one inch, but she had woven black silk so fine as to require 120 threads to the inch, or 4,320 to each yard, for which she would receive 4½d., or somewhere about 1d. for each 1,000 throws of the shuttle, to which must be added the time lost in picking, entering, and twisting the silk.

When these remarks were first published, we received a number of communications confirming their accuracy. One wrote thus:-

"In the name of the Spitalfields weavers, I humbly beg to offer you our sincere and heartfelt thanks for your exposition of our miserable condition. The few cases you noticed are undeniable and accurate, and though our trade abounds with similar instances, they were quite sufficient to show that the sufferings of the silk-weavers were no chimera. There are very few of the silk-weavers whose earnings, from Christmas to Christmas, average 10s. per week; very few indeed: they have so many drawbacks, and loss of time waiting for their work, besides the low price they receive for their labour, that it is really astonishing how many of them live.

"The zeal with which you advocate the interests of the working classes, and the improvement of their dwellings, is duly appreciated, and your services are gratefully acknowledged by them. You, sir, kindly but truly state that the weavers are mostly remarkable for intelligence : it is the more remarkable, when considered how scanty are their means to obtain it. They really have no time to improve their morality or intelligence. Even the Sunday brings no Sabbath to many of them : they know no change but from the loom to the bed, and from the bed to the loom. The weavers are considered by many who are without the least knowledge of their real condition, as an ignorant, discontented set of people, always making a noise, and never satisfied.

"These persons, sir, would do well to follow your example, by making a personal investigation; they would then be able to judge whether we have not sufficient cause for complaint. I think, sir, it would be difficult, if not impossible, in this country, to find a body of mechanics forced to toil so incessantly, and subsist in such penury as the silk-weavers, and whatever will be the end of this state of things (which cannot last much longer), I am at a loss to imagine. Hundreds of the silk-weavers would be but too glad to transfer their labours to other channels of industry, did the opportunity but offer itself. I have long been trying to find other means of employment myself. I am now only thirty-one years of age, and feel strong and active enough for any work; yet, being friendless, I have, like many others, failed in my endeavours. So I suppose we must struggle on in our hopeless condition a little longer, trusting to the hand of Providence to come to our rescue.

"Sir, it is seldom the true state of the Spitalfields weavers is brought to public notice: and they are all unanimous in giving you their thanks and heartfelt gratitude for your observations."

From one we received a poem of 112 lines, setting forth touchingly the melancholy condition of his family, and wrongfully attributing it to the parsimony and bad feeling of his employers. We cannot print the whole of the poem, but we will give some portions of it for more than one reason. The lines begin:-

"Life's to some a happy dream,
With smiling friends and pleasures gay,
With scarce a cloud to mar the scene,-
All brightness, like a summer's day.
The trials the struggling poor do feel
Are unknown to their breast;
The wrongs to which the low-born yield
Can ne'er disturb their rest
And many a noble heart has broke
Beneath its silent woe,
With heroism that bespoke
A greatness such as heroes show.
And I, the son of poverty,
What wretched sights I've seen,
Where want has held its sovereignty,

With visage haggard, lean.
Twas in a weaver's cheerless shop
Where first I saw the light;
The want of work had been our lot
T' increase our wretched plight."

The father, long out of work, at length obtains employment, and, according to the writer,-

"For thirteen years in slavish toil
He swelled their princely store,
For others wove the costly robe,
While threadbare clothes he wore.
From early morn till late at eve,
And oft till midnight hour,
Within his loom exhausted, weave
Till nature checked the power.
And when his trying task is done,
In fear he wends his way,
Lest in his wrath the heartless one
Should stop his scanty pay."
"His home-alas! scarce worth the name-
A room some few feet square,
With bed and loom crammed in one room,
And children huddled there.
With such a scene before one's eyes,
To be condemned to toil,
Half clothed, half fed,-much better dead
Beneath the peaceful soil."

Getting too old to weave, he is discharged ; and the writer reproaches the rich who wear the brocade for disregard of the want which prevails where it is made; and refers to, what we know to be the case, the honesty with which, spite of poverty, the employer's materials are preserved and returned.

We will not close our present chapter without repeating the appeal we made at the commencement of it in favour of the outcast children of London, who may be either good citizens or a pestilence, according as they are trained; and we would further say that "now is the time,-not to-morrow; "now is ours,-to-morrow may not be. Let us remember that "there is, in the smile of those whom we have served, a something which we may take with us into heaven.

CHAPTER VII.

THE statements in the previous chapters have had the advantage of a large circulation : the statements remain uncontradicted, the deductions unquestioned. And yet, if we are asked what practical good to any extent has up to this time resulted from them, we must, with shame, reply, - none-positively none!

And soon the cholera will be upon us. It passed as if by electrical agency over certain lands, almost depopulating places peculiarly circumstanced, and has made its way to London. At Newcastle-upon-Tyne and Gateshead it carried hundreds to the grave.

The authorities of these towns have been closing grave-yards, and cleansing lanes and alleys, which, for filth and neglect, we venture to say were not to be surpassed in the kingdom. *But why did they wait until the plague came!* Surely the intelligent and scientific men of Newcastle must have known what a magazine of dangerous material had been formed by their neglect, and which only wanted the touch to destroy hundreds of lives.

Are we to wait in London until the disease has again broken out among us, before proper measures are resorted to, to stop its course Surely this ought not to be so. London should at once undergo a systematic inspection, and be' put into a condition to resist the pestilence: we feel certain if this were done in a proper manner, it would lead to the most important results and benefits. It will be of no use, however, to send the beadles and such-like functionaries, but a staff of intelligent persons, who are capable of appreciating the peculiarities of the various means of death so plentifully strewed around the metropolis, and accustomed to these inquiries. Expense should not he considered: let the cost be what it may, it will produce a saving. Every vestry and board of guardians should at once initiate proceedings : every man should feel himself; as he is, personally interested in seeing them properly and effectually carried out. Many of the places which we have seen with our own eyes, cry shame on the institutions of the nineteenth century.

We would, however, on this, as on other occasions, restrain our expressions of feeling, and confine ourselves to some plain statements, which can be practically disposed of. Let us look again at one or two of the localities already illustrated and described by us as ready for any bad seed. Take, for example, the neighbourhood of "Paradise" (fallen), at King's-cross. A very active assistant in this inquiry went to that locality on one evening, in company of Mr. Sutherin, a surgeon of this neighbourhood, known for his zeal in the cause of the suffering poor.

The first place visited - a large yard surrounded by houses - contained about twenty cart-loads of oyster-shells, kept there in store for laying the foundations of roads. The smell of these was most offensive: the proprietor of the yard was out of the way, and his wife could not think how any one could complain of "clean oyster-shells," - forgetting that large particles of the fish adhered to each shell, and were left there to putrify. In another part of the yard was a stack, containing many cart-loads of cowhouse and stable refuse, piled up against the back wall of a house here (in this very house) the doctor had at the time a case of typhus fever.

The water comes in on Saturday night at six o'clock, and there is no more until *six o'clock on Monday night*. On Sunday night there was no water in this or the adjoining houses. In one of the houses, within a few yards of that attacked by fever, we learned, by the peculiar and dismal howl, that the Irish inmates were *"waking"* some one dead.

You may wander on amid scenes of dilapidation, and enter rooms with miserable atmospheres : it is a sad sight to see young and helpless infants in such places. To all our inquiries, "there was *no water last Sunday"* was the reply, and of course none during the greater part of Monday. There are numerous pig-styes, giving forth foul odours, close to the doors, and below the dwellings of the people, although it is contrary to law to allow these animals to be kept in populous towns. It is also illegal to stack up mountains of vegetables and other refuse; and as these illegal acts are the undoubted cause of many deaths, a heavy responsibility must rest on the guardians of parishes, whose duty it is to see the sanitary laws for the welfare of the poor carried into effect.

In a dilapidated house, thickly inhabited, and for which the inhabitants pay about £27 a year, the back-yard was disgraceful: a cesspool was overflowing and spreading over the ground, and deep pools of stagnant and poisonous matter filled the cracks of the pavement. No description can give an idea of this place. There was no water last Sunday, "not a drop of water in the next yard, nor in the next and the next." There are cesspools open or closed below and adjoining the houses. One or two streets have lately had drains made through them : in the large remainder all lies on the surface;- heaps of the refuse of piggeries, cowsheds, and stables, vegetables, fish, &c. - with bad pavement, great poverty, and for nearly two days in the week no water! Even the dumb animals-horses, cows, pigs, and asses, - must also be equally ill provided with this necessary. Such are the notes of a neighbourhood, which we venture to say is not much ex-eeded in ill condition amongst savages, and is certainly disgraceful to the parish of St. Pancras.

This "Paradise," and parts adjoining, are positively worse now than at the time of our first visit six or seven months ago. Let none regard our description as overcoloured. So far from this being the case, the abominations are underrated, and this we will prove by a few further categorical statements. We will commence with Pancras-place, Pancras-road. There are sixteen consecutive houses in this row in a most filthy and dilapidated state, as they have been for years. A person residing opposite to them informs us they have not been painted for thirty years: other say, they cannot remember them undergoing repair. Apparently, if one were taken down, they would all fall: in fact, they are not fit for human habitation. The cesspools are in a most offensive state, being only partly covered, so that the contents often rise over the boards which form the flooring. The stench is, as the occupiers observe, "horrible." These houses are mostly let to five or more families, each family occupying a room, for which they pay respectively, from the kitchen upwards, 3s., 2s. 9d., 1s. 6d., and 1s. per week, or at the rate of £29. 5s. per annum, for places not fit for pigs to dwell in.

In Weller's-court, a small court leading from old St. Pancras-road to Ashby-street, the houses were a few days ago in a most dilapidated state, the back-yards, as well as the court itself, disgusting and offensive, the soil from the cesspool actually overflowing, baskets of decaying fish strewed about, stagnant water and heaps of fish and dung lying about in all directions. Some of these houses have no convenience, so that offensive matter is thrown into corners, or deposited upon the heaps of dung that lie in various places. The effluvium evolved is most injurious to animal life, indeed worse than direct poison; for in the latter case, if you know the character of the poison, you have an antidote; while in the former, it is insidious in its effect, and is not apparent in many cases until too late for medical assistance to be of any avail. Ashby-street, commencing at the upper end of Weller's-court, and running parallel with St. Pancras-road, consists of about twenty-nine houses: most of them, particularly those on the further side from the road, are in a most dirty and filthy state, the cesspools in most instances full, and the smell exceedingly offensive. The street is without a drain, and strewed with animal and vegetable matter. Scarlet fever of a very malignant form, as well as small-pox, has been raging here. Let us look into a house in an adjoining street. This consists of five small rooms, and a back kitchen or washhouse, and is occupied by five families, numbering thirty-three individuals, distributed as follows, viz.-seven in the kitchen, which is underground, a man, his wife, and five children; seven in the room over the kitchen, a man, his mother, wife, and four children : in the room behind this are four labourers, who sleep upon two small beds, which fill the room eight in the top front room, a shoemaker, his wife, and six children seven in the top back room, six *men and women*, with one child, occupying only two beds. The kitchen is very dirty, has two sinks, both untrapped, communicating with the drain, and contains the water-butt for the supply of water to the several families. The house itself is filthy, the walls besmeared with dirt, and the yard contains an open cesspool and stagnant water. No wonder that cholera has already been busy in this house!

Being in this neighbourhood, let us mention a curious and instructive instance of the consequence of sanitary neglect which occurred not far off. In a narrow passage lined with houses, leading from Clarendon-square to the New-road, passengers that way may have noticed a small manufactory of yeast for the use of the London bakers. The owner of this place has always been a pattern of cleanliness : many have remarked the pleasant look of the old-fashioned little garden, the stone pavement so cleanly washed, forming "quite a picture." Opposite this place are stables for horses, in the possession of a greengrocer, who, in spite of remonstrance, stacks up his decayed vegetables in his yard. It is well known that all the processes of brewing require scrupulous attention to cleanliness, and that want of care in this respect is almost certain to stop fermentation. The manufacture of yeast is little different from the brewing of ale the ingredients are allowed to boil for a certain time : when that is done, and they are mixed, if the atmosphere is in a proper state, fermentation will go on. The accumulation of filth had become great in the yard opposite the yeast manufactory, and at the time of carting it away the smell was offensive. The yeast-brewer was at work, and instead of the fermentation going on as it ought, by covering the liquid with a thick, deep yellow coat of yeast, the surface was stagnant as ditch-water, and covered in parts with a blue mouldy-looking scum. On a similar occasion, the yeast-brewer seeing the fermentation nearly checked, removed the vessel of liquor through the garden to the back of his house, at a distance from the smell, and the brewing at once went on in a thriving manner. This seems a simple matter, but it may serve to bring to the minds of some who shut their eyes to the fact, that the air, although they do not *see* it, is a powerful agent : it can destroy the functions of life as surely, and in some cases as instantaneously, as a cannon-ball.

In a previous chapter we mentioned the condition of the "Coal-yard," at the top of Drury-lane,-a spot near which the Great Plague of 1665 first made its appearance. At a recent visit the place seemed even worse than formerly. At one end of these dwellings is a building occupied by the parish poor, and here a fire-engine is kept. At the, time of our visit, about eight o'clock on one Saturday evening, the people opposite this place complained of their neglected condition and inadequate supply of water. They had then none in their tank. Suddenly a cry of fire was raised, and the engine was brought forth for use. *"Thank God,"* said one of the women, *"there is a fire: we will soon get some water."* Presently the water ran into the empty cask, the turncock not being able to prevent it from coming into the houses' at the time he supplied the engines. Surely they *must* be ill supplied with water - one of the greatest necessaries of life - when they *"thank God for a fire."*

We could lay our finger on a map of London, and trace the districts which will be ravaged by cholera; and it is certain, by proper care and management, that the evil might be lessened, if not prevented altogether. Will it not be infamous if endeavours be not made?

It has been shown that the cholera can be battled with by sanitary measures, and that fever in the same way can be abated. The model lodging-house in Charles-street, Drury-lane, is a striking example of the advantages and effects of proper means in one of the worst neighbourhoods. This house has now been open about eight years, and is occupied by from seventy to eighty lodgers daily; and yet during that period, although cholera and fever have killed numbers on all sides, there has not been a single case of either in it. A good supply of water, proper drainage, and ventilation, have stopped disease; and it is not a little gratifying to find that the example of this building, in such a place, has not been without its effect on the landlords of the adjoining houses.

If, then, human life can thus be saved, the condition of houses becomes a matter demanding the care of all persons in authority, and they should at once put a stop to the species of wholesale murder now going on.

Early attention should be directed to the supply of water, the more so as the impression prevails that this is ample. Our readers already know how untrue this is, and we will add some further proofs. One evening, between six and eight o'clock, we examined Rose-street and the courts adjoining, with this object in view. Rose-street is near Covent-garden, with several narrow passages which lead to Long-acre, and is thickly inhabited by a poor, and in some instances bad class of people. Having before described many similar dwellings, we will not now enter into particulars in that respect, but content ourselves by stating that all we have written will only give a slight notion of their miserable condition. At No. 18, Rose-street, they said, "We don't have a drop of water on the Sunday; we have to go to Covent- garden. There are not so many people in the house now as at other times; they have gone to the hop-picking." There are eight rooms in this house, each let to separate families : although we did not get at the exact numbers, we may at the very least put the population, even at the present, at five in each room; that will give forty persons; the water-cask would contain 120 gallons, and is filled on each Saturday afternoon between three and four o'clock; there is then no further supply until Monday at about the same hour, - about forty-eight hours!

It will be seen that this supply is totally inadequate; but, says an inhabitant, "Go to the other house, sir; the poor craters there are actually starving for want of water." The premises in which these water-starved people live belong to eminent brewers. Inquire in this description of neighbourhood where you please, and the answer will be, "We have no water on Sunday; we are obliged to beg for it." "The poor creatures," said one, "do not know what to do for water on a Sunday; it is very troublesome, but one cannot refuse them water; bless you, they come begging and begging, until I am often without myself."

What is the condition of the drainage in this neighbourhood? we inquired of one who has a manufactory near - "Drain, sir? here is my drain," pointing to a wooden spout lying near the ground. "There's my drain, sir; it runs into the street there, on to the surface, and down through that court into the 'Acre.'"

Angel-court, Long-acre, is a wretched place. The six houses have one site for water, closet, and dust- heap, and here is a view of it (Fig. 8).

The place containing these conveniences for say 150 persons, is in a small yard or court. Here, the people state, they are not short of water; on inquiry, we found that there was a tank for the reception of water somewhere underground; we were unable to discover the exact position, but it is not likely to be far from the pump shown in the above engraving. Here there is nothing but surface drainage, and in consequence the refuse of the closet (A), &c. must pass into a cesspool, most probably in the neighbourhood of the subterranean water-tank.

Fig. 8.

It is a curious circumstance, and we have before alluded to it, that the people living in these places are slow to acknowledge the unwholesomeness of their condition. Inquire how their children are in health, and (although you may see disease written on their faded countenances) they will almost invariably say, "Quite well, thank God." Let those persons, however, whose business it is (or at least ought to be) to look into these houses, not be content with this off-hand reply. Let them inquire the number of times that fever has visited the family; how many friends they lost by the last attack of cholera; *how many children they have living, and* HOW MANY DEAD. The inference will be very different.

Wild-passage, Drury-lane, is a narrow court, thickly inhabited; and we may say in passing, that this and other neighbourhoods in London are certainly more densely populated since the dispersion of persons in other places by the Lodging-house Act, and the removal of numerous dwellings without any suitable provisions being made, than they were before.

Here is a drawing (Fig. 9) of a water-cask in Wild-passage, which reminds us of the withered condition of the ship graphically described by Coleridge: and let it be remembered that this vessel is provided for a house of eight families.

Fig. 9.

In this place the people say they have "a very bad supply of water," "on Sundays have no water at all," "have to hunt for it on Sundays, and even in the week days are often without water." In one house they had had no water for six weeks. In another house we found the water-cask, dust-bin, and closet in a cellar. The underground arrangement of water- cask or tank, closet, and dust-bin, cannot be too much reprobated; it is unwholesome in the extreme. Several persons, not only here but also in Rose-street, occupy cellars. One woman in Wild-passage said that she had been driven by poverty and distress to rent an underground back-kitchen or cellar, for herself and three children, for 1s. per week, and that they had all been laid up at one time with fever, but recovered.

In the neighbourhood of Marlborough-street police station, Berwick-street, a district already referred to, there is no water in the courts and alleys on the Sundays. Here many of the people complain, not only that the water-casks are deficient in size, but that the water is frequently turned off before the cask is full. In one of these little courts, the people hearing us make inquiries respecting the water, rushed out from all sides, speaking with bitter rage of the inadequate provision. We managed to gather, amid the din, that they suspected a person who keeps a small general shop (one of those curiously squalid attempts at trading met with in these neighbourhoods), and through which the water-pipe passed, of "thieving the water on the way to them. On examining the shop, we found that the shopkeeper had bored a small hole in the water-pipe, to prevent him, as he said, from struggling and fighting with the people in the court when the water came in, "there being so many of them, and so little water, that they were often like so many devils."

We are simply telling a plain tale, and have used unvarnished facts, in the hope that our observations may at the present time direct attention to the water supply amongst the poor. It is a matter of necessity and justice, which should be attended to even without consideration of the cholera. ·Water should be supplied, if not constantly, at least every day, Sunday of course included; the receptacles should be examined, covers should be put to them, secured by locks, and the water should be removed as far as possible from the closets and dust-bins.

One more fact before we conclude. The cholera killed at one time 100 persons a day at Newcastle, where the population is about 90,000. If it attack the metropolis with similar violence, and the mortality bear here the same proportion to the population as at Newcastle, we should lose 20,000 persons in a week, or *double the number of the soldiers who were encamped at Chobham!*

We say this not as ground for alarm, but as a reason for preparation; and we again exhort all who have power, immediately to take those steps by which, under Providence, as science amid experience show conclusively, the evil may be mitigated, if not altogether averted.

CHAPTER VIII.

DIRTY, dilapidated, and unwholesome dwellings destroy orderly and decent habits, degrade the character, and conduce to immorality. Bad air produces feelings of exhaustion and lowness of spirits, and these tempt to the use of stimulants-the fruitful parents of all crime. We have urged and re-urged this in many shapes: but repetition is necessary, improvement moves so slowly. The "New Lodging-house Act" is being pushed gradually yet firmly into use, and is, without doubt, effecting much good. "The sanitary policemen," as the earl of Shaftesbury said on a recent occasion, "are looked upon by the poor as guardian angels." Admitting the genera] good of this measure, there is, nevertheless, one consideration which requires careful and immediate attention. While the new Act of Parliament is driving the poor from their close quarters, we say now, as we have said before, no adequate provision has been made for their reception elsewhere, and the consequence must be that rent for dwellings will be raised beyond the means of the destitute poor, *particularly those with families of children,* and they will simply remove *the overcrowding* to places not at present discovered by the police, or be compelled to seek shelter in the workhouses.

The following case shows the operations of the Act in this respect :-A widow, very poor, with three children, the eldest ten years of age, is charged 3s. 6d. a week for lodging in a house in "Short's-gardens," Drury-lane: this is an amount of weekly rent which it is totally out of the power of this woman, in her present circumstances, honestly to pay. The lodging-house keeper says that having known the woman for some years, he has, since his house was licensed, let her and the children sleep there for 3s. 6d. a week-a sum less than he ought to charge: the ordinary charge would be 4*d.* a night for the mother (2s. 4*d.* a week), and half-price for the children (3s. 6d. a week); in all, 5*s.* 10d. This is a startling amount of rent, but the lodging-house keeper, as he observed, since he dare not admit more than a certain number of inmates, must charge the amount allowed by law to enable him to live, and at the same time pay his rent and taxes.

Immediate and large provision of lodgings is required by the present condition of things, particularly for the very poor who have families of children.

Lodgings of a certain description are needed where a man or woman with a family of children can be sheltered at a cost of from 1s. 6d. to 2s. a week. The City of London should do something to supply this want. In all directions they are demolishing the dwellings which are at all likely to afford shelter to the poorest, and are driving poverty, vice, and ignorance out of the City. Yet, the "poor will not cease to be in the land," and as it is evident that those who formerly lodged, and are at the present time living within the City, must otherwise go elsewhere; the effect of this will be to burden the surrounding parishes with the pauperism which they have turned from their own doors. We would gladly behold this demolition if other provisions were made; and it is to be hoped that the Corporation of London, under these circumstances, will set an example in trying if wholesome shelter for poor families can or can not be provided, remuneratively, at the cost to which we have alluded, viz, from 1s. 6d. to 2s. a week. We do not care about the old-fashioned style of house being followed, but would wish that buildings should be erected on a strictly economical principle, dictated by the superior scientific knowledge of the present day; and we are satisfied that places of this description could be reared, which, by judicious arrangements, might be made not only profitable to the builders, but at the same time to confer a great service on the whole community.

The importance of showing that suitable dwellings and other accommodations for the industrious poor can be made self-supporting, induces us to mention the last annual report of the Metropolitan Association for the Improvement of the Dwellings of the Poor, particularly as we are of opinion that buildings erected for English working men must not be institutions of charity. Satis6ed as we are that a sufficient provision of healthful habitations for the working classes can only he hoped for as the result of commercial speculation; and anxious as we have ever been, therefore, to show that capital may be advantageously invested in providing these, we are much interested in the success of the Metropolitan Association.

At first the dividend paid was small, necessarily, because, amongst other reasons, while the houses were building, of course there was no return from the capital expended: at the present moment, however, as we are glad to hear, all the buildings are paying about five per cent. "Once let it be proved," as Lord Carlisle said some time ago, "that the act of doing good, in however unpretending and commonplace a manner, to large masses of the struggling and impoverished, would pay its own way, and insure its fair profit, and it would follow that benevolence, instead of being only an ethereal influence in the breasts of a few, fitful and confined in its operations, would become a settled, sober habit of the many ; widening as it went, occasioning its own rebound, and adding all the calculations of prudence to all the impulses of generosity.

The Metropolitan Buildings, St. Pancras-road, which cost £17,700, produces about £1,000 a year, and pays well In a sanitary point of view, the results are most satisfactory. Dr. Southwood Smith has shewn that the average rate of mortality in the improved dwellings, erected by the Metropolitan Association, is not one-third that of the metropolis generally, while the rate of infant mortality in the same dwellings is little more than one-fifth. When the various expenses of procuring an Act of Parliament, the necessary expenses of management, the amount of capital not put to remunerative use, together with the losses on the other buildings, and which can be traced to certain causes, are considered, we think that the St. Pancras building holds out fair promise to any capitalist who, without Acts of Parliament, &c. could place similar buildings in proper localities. The Report of the Society for Improving the condition of the Labouring Classes proves the same fact.

We were much shocked by the intensely ignorant condition of the children in Short's-gardens. Those whom we questioned, about nine or ten years of age, could not read, and said they had "never heard of God." A dog-fight produced a scene such as we will not attempt to describe-a scene miserably sad: heads were in every window, and the dilapidated quarter seemed filled with vicious life. As the place, so the people. The yard in which the scene occurred was strewed with vegetables and other refuse; it -was Saturday night, and the dust-heap was overflowing; the pavement was broken, and contained pools of unwholesome water; the whole place was filthy in the extreme.

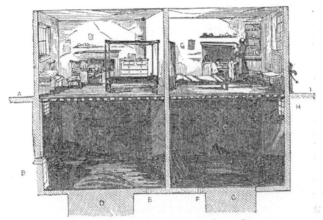

Fig. 10.—Living-rooms with Cesspools beneath.

The formation of sewers in this neighbourhood now going on is hailed with gratitude by the inhabitants. Some time ago we referred to the cesspools in use here, and we will assist that description by a diagram which exhibits the condition of many houses in other places besides Drury-lane. The drains run in at A, B: D and G are the cesspools: the overflow is pumped away at H. C, C, are dark cellars: a drain connecting the two cesspools: with gratings at E and F. A whole volume of description would not speak so forcibly.

A supply of water in the poorer neighbourhoods on *Sundays,* particularly during the summer months, is greatly needed. At present, the water is generally turned on on Saturdays at about three o'clock in the afternoon, and no further supply is to be had until the middle of the following Monday. In hundreds of instances the water-tank is quite inadequate for the numerous families surrounding it, and many have no vessels for water in their own dwellings; the consequence is, that in most cases the supply is soon exhausted, and the people in these places are not only left without the means of washing their hands and face on the Sabbath-day, but actually have "not a drop to drink."

A little to the north of Hatton-garden and Leather-lane is a neighbourhood of the worst description, and which certainly requires some interference. Nearly opposite Hatton-garden this populous and dirty place is reached by steep descents, opposite Leather-lane, by a flight of steps. The latter brings us to the first platform, if we may so call it: here are two long rows of houses, with courts leading from them. These courts, as in fact are most of the neighbouring houses, are occupied by the Irish and others engaged in Leather-lane market. One of them in particular we found in a shocking condition. A tank for water was placed, for the convenience of the numerous inhabitants, in such a position as to render the water impure in a few hours; but on Monday, at one o'clock, there was no water in the cistern, nor had there been *a drop for the accommodation of scores of pent-up women and children since Saturday evening*. On Saturday, at three o'clock in the afternoon, the water is turned on, and, as we are told, continues to run for rather more than half an hour. The inhabitants rush out, and such of them as have any vessels contrive to fill them, after a struggle, which suggests to the beholder the arrival of parched travellers at a spring in the desert. Many, however, have nothing which will hold a sufficient quantity of water; and even in the case of those who have, the water, after remaining in a room occupied by many persons, surrounded by impurities, must be rendered unwholesome before the Sunday morning. By that time the water has become precious. The costermongers return late on the Saturday night or early on Sunday morning, and require a supply of water to render themselves, after their dirty work, decent and comfortable on the Sunday. This, in the present state of things, is generally impossible. "I cannot be clean if I would," -a poor young wife said to us. She was certainly not *nineteen*, but had a baby in her arms and one about two years old by her side!

When we visited the place the dust-bin was full, and the pavement strewed with vegetables and other refuse. The state of the exterior was so bad, that it was unnecessary to enter the dwellings in order to understand their condition. Here, King Fever and his friendly potentate, Cholera, may revel in all their terrors. And remember, this place is in the midst of London.

Lucy's-buildings, another portion of this district, is singularly well adapted for the purpose of destroying health : continuing from the steps from the end of Leather-lane, and crossing at a steep gradient the street already alluded to, we come to three double rows of buildings, each containing twelve houses (rent, 3s. 3d. a week) of three rooms each. The lowest court is reached by nine steps : at the top of the steps is a sort of narrow back-yard, in which are conveniences, one for each two houses. Nothing can be worse than this arrangement,-hut we cannot go into details. The backs of the rooms built against this bank are damp, and most unfavourable to health. In the lower court is an untrapped gully-hole, which is also most offensive : here cholera was a visitor, and fever seems to be held in terror. The water- cistern was empty on Saturday evening, and would continue so until Monday afternoon. This court, badly as it is situated, might be materially improved in condition by two things, viz, an unlimited supply of water, and the application of proper traps to the closets and gully-holes.

Pursuing this point, namely, the supply of water, we started on a voyage of examination, and in more than fifty houses, entered between the hours of two and four o'clock in the afternoon of one Friday, there was *not a drop of water!*

In Charlotte's-buildings, Gray's-Inn-lane, a place swarming with people, there were not three gallons of water at six o'clock on Saturday afternoon.

For those, then, who say our general subject is too vast for them to touch, here is a simple, practicable point for their operations,-a supply of water for the poor on Sunday mornings.

Many unwholesome parts of London in the fashionable west-in Mary-le-bone, in Bloomsbury, &c.-are hidden behind the large squares, and in passages leading from good streets. These little "Rookeries" are so numerous, and individually of such small extent, that our space prevents us from giving more than two or three examples.

In Great Coram-street, leading from Tavistock-square, close to the Russell Institution, is a narrow, squalid-looking turning, Little Coram-street, running north to Tavistock-place. A stranger visiting this street will not fail to be struck with the immense number of children, women, and others, who swarm in crowds evidently too great for the visible houses. A careful inspection shows narrow passages leading from this street to collections of small houses inhabited by very poor people. One of these courts (Coram-place) *is fifteen feet below the surface of the street,* and is reached by a flight of steps. Having said this much, and considering the poverty of many of the inhabitants, and the ill-condition of the houses, none will wonder at bad results. Surrounded on all sides by tall buildings, and planted below the surface of the ground, it is scarcely possible for a breath of even comparatively pure air to reach the inhabitants.

In the map in "Chamberlain's London," dated 1770 (only eighty-four years ago), all this district is marked fields, the farthest houses on the north being Ormond-street, Queen-square, Southampton-place, and the British Museum. The Foundling Hospital, with the burial-ground at the back, was an isolated building.

By the way, we wonder how many persons, not living in this neighbourhood, know what is called "the Colonnade," running out of Grenville-street, Brunswick-square, parallel with Bernard-street and Guildford-street,-a row of about forty houses (about 500 feet in extent), where the one-pair floor projects and is carried on a row of wooden columns, with a raised walk beneath, over the basement, in front of shops on the ground-floor, like the "Rows" in Chester? The effect is singular. We are dealing, however, with more serious matters than *appearances*.

In a narrow street leading from the south side of Clipston-street is a place very similar to the courts mentioned above. From this street two passages lead to underground courts; on one side by a flight of steps; on the other, by a steep descent. Their condition is so similar to that of the courts we have just described, that it is unnecessary to enter into particulars, except to say that there is no proper drain, and that in the court on the right-hand side is a cesspool, belonging to some of the neighbouring houses, the contents of which flow through the flag-stones of the court. Some of the women are afraid to trust their children to play there, lest the covering should fall in, and they be suffocated in the receptacle.

Any one taking the trouble to inquire into this matter will not fail to be surprised at the little knowledge the persons living in these places have of their unhealthiness. In answer to the questions as to the health of their family, they usually reply, "It is very good, except at times." The appearance of the children generally contradicts this statement; and if you inquire of a person who has had a large family the number living, the answer too often shows a sad amount of loss. One woman, whom we thus questioned in this court, where she had lived twenty-three years, had had thirteen children, and but three were then alive.

Since the first publication of our observations on the amazing number of children now in the streets of London who are being educated in vice,-forbidden from good, and prepared for a life of misery, - as we then ventured to say, Lord Shaftesbury has brought into the House of Peers a Bill to meet part of the evil. Earnestly we hope it may do so; but in the meanwhile individuals should remember how much is in their own power m their several districts, and not to leave all to an Act of Parliament. Let us each

"LIVE FOR SOMETHING."

CHAPTER IX.

SANITARY and municipal reforms make but slow progress. The London streets were in former days thronged with thieves; scores of peaceable London citizens were robbed, often beaten, and sometimes murdered, and this practice might have continued if the thieves had not made an unsuccessful attempt to rob the queen, and succeeded in robbing a London alderman. Then regular patrols were put on the streets, lights were hung out, and numbers of the robbers hanged. In other instances we find a handful of interested individuals, having influence, continuing certain evil practices, until pestilence or some other interference of Providence alarms them personally, or they are forced into alteration by the strong voice of public opinion.

The "grave-yard" question was a few years since ably and resolutely agitated by Mr. Walker, assisted by nearly all the ability of the London and provincial press; circumstances of the most revolting nature were placed before the public; and, although seemingly beyond belief, have never been contradicted. Soon after these matters were made known, the cholera paid us a visit, alarming the minds of men by the fierceness of its visitation; many reforms were determined upon, amongst others, the immediate discontinuance of intramural interments: this desirable boon then seemed a certainty which every one might congratulate himself upon. Notwithstanding this hopeful appearance, the grave-yard question is even now scarcely settled. We will not give to any credit for common sense, - we will not give them credit for common honesty, if they say it is right that a monstrous heap of decaying mortality should be placed amongst the living, and opened week by week, perhaps day by day, to receive additions to the mass, and to emit in more concentrated form its destructive gases. Whether the remains be those of rich or poor, all must decompose to the elements that form the human body, which are indestructible, and these must be dispersed throughout the neighbourhood.

But why argue a matter which has again and again been determined? No one will be bold enough to say that the practice is wholesome, christianlike, or proper, and all must earnestly desire its abandonment, if not personally interested in its maintenance. Our large cities are rapidly doubling their population. We live in the times of railways, the steam printing-press, and the electric telegraph; old-fashioned and half measures will only end in disappointment, and eventually in greater sacrifices. The whole system of intramural interments should be at once changed. ·*Let* us have no more cemeteries in our streets, even if only one-third filled and "agreeable places;" let us add no more to the stacks of coffins which fill the vaults of chapels and churches; but provide proper places at a distance from towns. Not long since the burial-grounds of St. James's in the Hampstead-road, St. Pancras', St. Giles's, and St. Martin's, were in pleasant fields. Look at them now! - plague-spots in the midst of thousands of people.

Fig. 11.—St. Pancras' Burial-ground.

The appearance presented by the ground of Old St. Pancras's parish is very extraordinary. Unaided imagination would scarcely reach to it, and we have therefore pencilled down its general aspect. An account of the number of bodies here deposited would startle the most apathetic.

St. Pancras' ground is truly a distressing sight. The stones - an assembly of reproachful spirits - are falling all ways; the outbuildings put up on its confines are rent, and the paved pathways are everywhere disrupted, such is the loose and quaking state of the whole mass. The practice of pit-burial is still continued in this ground. When we were there last, we found a hole with six coffins in it, waiting its complement of about double that number!

Fig. 12.

St. Giles's ground, the soil of which is a stiff clay, was in a disgusting state, - a mere mud-pond in that portion which is appropriated to the burial of the poor.

Parts of the London burial-grounds which have been properly "worked," as they call it, are filled from a depth of about 13 feet up to 3 or 4 feet from the surface; our readers may see by a reference to the annexed engraving (Fig. 12) of the surface of St. Giles's-in-the-Fields, that the graves are dug as nearly as possible side by side. A full-sized grave would be from 6 feet 3 inches to 6 feet 6 inches in length; the measurement we made of the raised tops of these graves showed them not more than 4 feet 6 inches in length. A square portion of the graveyard is appropriated for present use; the 4 feet 6-inch graves soon become less, and speedily are not to be recognised by the friends of the deceased. A flat space is soon made for fresh graves, which are dug, of course, not so deep, and thus the ground is "managed" until no more coffins can find room. We need not ask if three or four feet of loose earth, and slight wooden coffins, will contain the fluids and gases of which these bodies are composed. These, quickly liberated, pass into the air and do their evil work.

The retention of burial-places in the midst of the living is a costly wickedness and a national disgrace.

Lord Palmerston some time ago addressed a letter to the Edinburgh Presbytery of the Scottish Church, in reply to their inquiry if a national fast would be appointed on account of the re-appearance of cholera, - which ought to have attention in every town-council, parish vestry, and private house throughout the kingdom.

"The Maker of the Universe," says the Home Secretary, "has established certain laws of nature for the planet in which we live, and the weal or woe of mankind depends upon the observance or the neglect of those laws. One of those laws connects health with the absence of those gaseous exhalations which proceed from overcrowded human beings, or from decomposed substances, whether animal or vegetable; and these same laws render sickness the almost inevitable consequence of exposure to those noxious influences. But it has, at the same time, pleased Providence to place it within the power of man to make such arrangements as will prevent or disperse such exhalations, so as to render them harmless; and it is the duty of man to attend to those laws of nature, and to exert the faculties which Providence has thus given to man for his own welfare."

The recent visitation of cholera the writer views as a warning that the people have neglected this duty, and that those persons with whom it rested to purify towns and to remove the causes of disease, have not been sufficiently active. "Lord Palmerston would, therefore, suggest, that the best course which the people of this country can pursue, to deseive that the further progress of the cholera should be stayed, will be to employ the interval that will elapse between the present time and the beginning of next spring in planning and executing measures by which those portions of their towns and cities which are inhabited by the poorest classes, and which, from the nature of things, must most need purification and improvement, may be freed from those causes and sources of contagion which, if allowed to remain, will infallibly breed pestilence and be fruitful in death, in spite of all the prayers and fastings of an united but inactive nation."

Excellent advice! The cholera is proceeding in London in its fatal course: death appears in the old spot; and under the usual insanitary conditions, and the measures adopted are not yet equal to the emergency. Foremost amongst the steps urgently required, we would place the removal and avoidance of cesspools; the closing of graveyards; and arrangements for the speedy and proper burial of the dead. It is often stated that the poorer classes, particularly the Irish, delight in filth, and would not live in properly conditioned houses if they could have them for the same money they pay for worse: it has been mentioned that whitewashing has been refused by some, and violence offered against improvement by others. We admit the frightful amount of ignorance amongst more than the very poor. How can it be otherwise, born and reared as they have been? Experience, however, tells us that in ninety-nine cases out of a hundred the poor have not the means of rising out of their filth and degradation. They are bound down to dirt. Still we have generally found the poor open to suggestions, willing to have the condition of things explained, and mostly anxious to escape, if it were possible, from the dens which it has been our painful duty to describe. The managers of public baths and washhouses will bear out this statement, but say at the same time that they have not yet reached the very poor: many have not even the small means required to go to these places, and more are ashamed to show their rags in the presence of others. It cannot be doubted that the poorer Irish require a peculiar kind of management, and it would be generally useless to attempt to interfere by apparent force with the forms in which they believe: let us, however, relate an instance which shows that reasoning and a kind way of putting the truth will receive attention.

A fatal case of cholera occurred at the end of 1852 in Ashby-street, close to the "Paradise" of King's-cross - a street without any drainage, and full of cesspools. This death took place in the back parlour on the ground floor abutting on the yard containing a foul cesspool and untrapped drain, and where the broken pavement, when pressed with the foot, yielded a black, pitchy, half liquid matter in all directions. The inhabitants, although Irish, agreed to attend to all advice given to them as far as they were able, and a coffin was offered to them by the parish. They said that they would like to wait until the next morning (it was on Thursday evening that the woman died), as the son was anxious, if he could raise the money, to bury his mother himself; but they agreed, contrary to their custom on such occasions, to lock up the corpse at twelve o'clock at night, and allow no one to be in the room. On Friday, the day after death, the woman was buried, and so far it was creditable to these poor people, since they gave up their own desires and customs, which bade them retain the body.

Is what followed equally creditable to the arrangements in St. Pancras? We think not. This corpse was brought to old St. Pancras graveyard, when, will it be believed, it was actually placed near the top of a pit twenty feet deep, containing two rows of full-grown coffins, which from time to time had been lodged there until the pile reached within a few feet of the surface. The effluvium from this pit was abominable : children were packed into the corners, so that not an inch of ground might be lost; and here during Saturday all this pitful of dead bodies, some of whom had, perhaps, fallen by fever and small-pox, together with the woman who had died of cholera, were left without a sprinkling of earth upon them. *On the Saturday afternoon the hole remained uncovered, waiting for more.* Probably on Sunday the complement was obtained and the heap was made complete; and then a few spadefuls of soil would be thrown over this mass of corruption to hide it from sight. Surely not a day should be lost in putting a stop to such disgraceful and dangerous proceedings. Who can, with justice, find fault with the improvidence and obstinacy of the poor when we see such doings on the part of those who are in authority, and ought to be better informed?

With respect to the cesspool system in the metropolis, all who inquire into the subject must be struck by the enormous magnitude of the evil. The number of cesspools allowed to remain, even in neighbourhoods where sewers have been formed, is extraordinary. None but those who have examined the subject can appreciate either the extent, or the sad consequences to health resulting from it. The excuses for this state of things are numerous. "Cesspools are certainly not right," says one, "and no doubt the drains below the kitchens smell very badly now and then; but my landlord is a very decent fellow; I have lived here some time, and I don't care to put him to expense;" or "My landlord's lease has not long to run, and he won't do anything." Some are in arrears of rent, and cannot remove. Others have established a business, or find their houses in some way suitably situated for sub-letting, and near their employment ; while *many are utterly ignorant of the extent of ill-health resulting from imperfect drainage;* and but few, comparatively, know that by an Act of Parliament passed in 1848 (11 & 12 Vict. c. 123), any offensive cesspool, &c. can be removed by the parish authorities upon receipt of a notice, in writing, signed by two inhabitant-householders. Cesspools ought at once to be got rid of in all neighbourhoods in which a sewer exists. This is a matter which not only affects the poor, but those above them in the social scale.

Many will remember houses of large size and respectable condition in which an atmosphere dull and heavy seems to hang in a substantial form. It is palpable and distinct. However cheerful a person may be at his entrance into one of these places, he will feel his spirits chilled and his whole system depressed. The smell is not of an acute description, but produces similar effects to those caused by a prolonged visit to one of our London crypts thickly occupied by the dead. Hundreds of houses in even good streets are thus circumstanced.

Persons residing not only in London, but in other large towns, who have not taken the trouble to understand the formation and ill effects of improper house-drains, wonder at the deadly air which fills their apartments, particularly in the evening, when doors and windows are closed, and the air within the house rarefied. We sometimes hear of persons smoking tobacco, as they say, "to purify the air," but this is only disguising the poison:- dressing the skeleton : the bones are within. We go into many houses which are positively shocking, and where, nevertheless, the smell is scarcely regarded by the inhabitants. The children are pale, and have no appetite; the older - occupants anxious and weary, with wide-open eyes, and closed mouth. To them everything looks black : the world is a prison. There are thousands in this beautiful world who do not know what a cheerful, pleasant home is: fault-finding and lamentation are their chief pleasures: and we verily believe that this number would be very considerably lessened by simply filling up the cesspool, and brightening up the house.

The history of London from an early period to the present time is a continued account of "trimming" measures, either forced by plague and pestilence, by fire, by interest, or by fears for the safety of property. An alderman is robbed, then the lighting of the City is seen after; an epidemic disease carries off one sixth of the old inhabitants, the Fleet Ditch is partly covered. In modern days the cholera pays us a visit, and during the terrors of its visitation the people are made to see and appreciate the unwholesomeness of intramural interments.

Up to this time, the slaughtering of animals is continued in the City and suburbs. In these particulars, London is worse than before the time of Henry VII.; for then, under payment of a heavy penalty, butchers were obliged to kill animals used for food at a distance from the inhabitants. We also, at the present day, tolerate the slaughtering of horses, &c., the preparation of tallow, and allow other abominations to be carried forward in the midst of a dense population.

In many parts of this great metropolis, often hidden from public view by stately squares and other buildings, lurk dense masses of houses totally unfit for human use, and yet crowded with those who, born in such localities, have little other prospect except the hospital, the workhouse, or the jail : here light or water scarcely enters, and instruction, save that in vice, is an almost utter stranger.

Is it not possible to provide dwellings for the abject poor of London and other large towns, where they may have light and the means of cleanliness, without appealing to charity for the supply of such buildings? It is said by many, that buildings on a new plan would not meet the views of those who have been reared in filth, and prejudiced by ignorance of their own good. We think that this prejudice, if the proper material were supplied, would soon vanish. Nothing can be more encouraging than the success of the first building erected in Old St. Pancras-road, by the Metropolitan

Association for Improving the Dwellings of the Industrious Classes, on the principle of the Edinburgh and Parisian houses. This departure from established custom met, at first, with many objectors, and some difficulty was felt in obtaining tenants. Since the opening of this building the rents have been twice raised, and, notwithstanding, it is rare now to meet with a set of rooms vacant. The inhabitants have continued to increase in respectability, and consist now of die-sinkers, engravers, ornamental painters, compositors, and skilled carpenters: in addition to these, we may mention a gentleman who has been for many years connected with literature, and a bank clerk. This first erection of the association is paying a handsome per centage on the expended capital; and it is almost certain that similar buildings, scattered about St. Pancras and elsewhere, would be a satisfactory speculation; and would also gradually pave the way to an alteration for the better of the dwellings of the very poor. We will not enter into the consideration of the slow progress of sewer reform; the necessity for the appointment of sanitary police, particularly in the districts of St. Pancras, Marylebone, Westminster, and parts of the Borough; but we cannot refrain from saying a few additional words respecting the "Grave-yard" question and the smoke nuisance. Many consider that, as an Act of Parliament has been passed, the evil of intramural interments in London has ceased. Such, however, is, unfortunately, not the case. On Sundays, during the afternoon, the St. Pancras-road and adjoining streets present the appearance of an almost continuous procession of coffins of children and adults, accompanied by the usual mourners, wending their way to the already closely-packed grave-yards of St. Pancras and St. Giles-in-the-fields. The scenes at these burial-grounds on Sundays are not very creditable. Who knows how soon the pestilence may again come upon us? The earth all over England is saturated by most unusual moisture, and the London grave-yards are completely drenched. This moisture must be extracted into the atmosphere and spread around. Who can foresee the consequence?

And now a few words as to another shadow, - smoke.

Smoke is a more tangible opponent to fight against than some people think. "It will all end in smoke, is a common expression to describe something which is, after all, nothing. This is a great mistake. Smoke is not nothing: it is a something which the public find it very difficult to get rid of, - an obvious, avoidable evil, - one of our disgraces.

The innocent animals sketched from nature, and placed here, are the one polluted, and the other astonished.

Fig. 13.

A stranger clean from the country.   *An inhabitant of Hyde-park.*
Yokel (*in alarm*).—*" Thou beest wondrous grim, sure !"*
Londoner.—*" To this complexion ewe must come at last."*

If, however, the country sheep wonders at the blackness of his neighbour, how much more must the sheep of experience be astonished (himself living in the neighbourhood of the court) to find by comparison with the coat of his new friend, fresh from verdant plains, the blackness of his own. Our sheep, perhaps, has a power of observation, and may consider that if this amount of blackness attach thus to the coat of wool, his daily food (the peculiarly-coloured grass of the London parks) must not be altogether wholesome: he will also consider the nature of the air thus loaded with large and distinct flakes of soot, visible to the eye, and think of unwholesome matter swallowed into his lungs, and that to an extent which could only be fully understood by comparison with the country atmosphere, by the display of collected particles, or by means of the microscope.

If sheep cannot thus estimate the effects of London smoke, at all events we can, and must view with horror delicate children and invalids, and indeed people of any sort, to the extent of two millions and a half and upwards, put in and obliged to breathe, not only the pestilent airs of bad drainage, and other matters to which we have often referred, but also the sooty atmosphere which the Hyde-park sheep illustrate.

The soot of the metropolitan chimneys is injurious in various ways. It injures to a certain extent the health of every one. It tinges with its duskiness the palace and the hovel: it coats and spoils the works of our painters and sculptors: it disfigures the works of architects; and it causes a large unnecessary expenditure in washing. Have we no chivalry in this practical age? Cannot the knights of the present time manage to relieve the ladies of Britain from an evil greater than were the dragons and enchantments of the times past?

There are some startling statistics on record touching the effect of London smoke: we have made some calculations of touching import to all who pay washing-bills, and which show that the damage done to clothes and furniture by our smoke is immense,-enough to astonish any one who has not thought seriously on the subject, and also enough, considering how particularly this evil presses on the female portion of the community, from the highest to the lowest, to stir up amongst us the latent spirit of chivalry already alluded to. Down with the Smoke! That is, let us never allow it to go up.

Smoke, it has been often shown, can be avoided, and the appearance and atmosphere of London may be completely altered. Ascend the principal tower of the Crystal Palace, at Sydenham, in the middle of the day, and all London lies shrouded in a dense haze, although at four in the morning from the same spot you may see every church in the metropolis; the City churches ranging in long rows, St. Paul's, Primrose-hill, Highgate and Hampstead, the Queen's Palace, Westminster Abbey; in fact, all the materials which form this great abode of humanity are distinctly in view, as distinctly almost as a scene in Italy or on the Rhine. London *"gets up;"* and then the gas-works, the brewers, the bakers, and various other manufacturers, as well as the good housewife, soon, by their united exertions, envelop London in a cloud which can be seen hanging over it for miles off like a sable pall or a sad thought.

If any of our country readers not living in manufacturing towns, such as Manchester, Birmingham, Leeds, Newcastle-on-Tyne, and some other places, think that our illustration of the Hyde-park sheep is too highly coloured, let them, if they happen to visit London, remember the condition of clean shirts and gloves after a day's use in the country, and compare them with those used at their metropolitan visit: let them also look at their hands and face: wash as often as they choose, the water will be of such a distinct blackness that no mistake can possibly be made respecting the extent and properties of London smoke.

If, however, London is so grim, what is the condition of Manchester, Leeds, and the banks of "Coally Tyne?" The accompanying sketch of Manchester when they are getting the steam up will be recognised by all strangers who have visited that great seat of industry. We remember meeting with a Londoner in the latter town who was almost speechless with astonishment at the numerous and immense volumes of smoke pouring out from all quarters-an effect only to he understood by actual observation.

Without pursuing the inquiry further, let us add that the quantity of coal now yielded by our coal-fields is called 32,000,000 tons annually, of which about 3,500,000 tons in the year are brought to London. It would not be difficult to estimate how much of this is wasted by our present unscientific mode of burning it, and is sent off, in the shape of very finely divided carbon, to contaminate the air, shorten the duration of daylight, and destroy property. That these evils may be avoided is certain, and it is much to be desired that manufacturers and others should not wait for legislative enactments, but should forthwith direct their attention to the subject, satisfied that although there may at first be practical difficulties in the way, these may all be overcome, not only with immense advantage to the public, but pecuniary gain to themselves.

Fig. 14.—Getting up the Steam.

CHAPTER X.

If we knock often, we shall be heard at last. In a lecture given at the London Hospital recently, Dr. Parker, after tracing the history of cholera, and showing that it was now following its former track, but that its ravages had been everywhere greater, said (and was fully entitled to say it),- We still hear men urge the impotence of our science to deal with the plague as a reproach against our profession. But no culpable neglect-no disgraceful ignorance-is ours. We cannot, indeed, stay the hand of the destroying angel-we cannot snatch his victim from the icy embraces of grim death-we cannot bid the already stagnant blood to flow onward in its course; but if the repeated warnings of members of our body had been heeded-if their reiterated exhortations and earnest remonstrances had been regarded - if their wise counsel had been followed, and the measures which they urged on the authorities of this land had been carried out, there are strong reasons for believing that cholera would not again have invaded our shores. Let us, then, remember that pestilence still rages in our densely-populated cities; that the deadly emanations from those plague-spots, the burial-grounds, still saturate the air of this metropolis with their pestiferous gases; that animal, and even human putrescence, still contaminates our water ; that fever still decimates our overcrowded emigrant-ships; that our poor still lodge in wretched hovels which are a disgrace to a civilised community; that lunatics are in many instances still treated as criminals; and that a comprehensive and efficient scheme of national education is still to be framed. Let us remember all these wants of the age, and not rest until the final victory be achieved.

Every day shows more and more strikingly that the cholera can be defeated by sanitary precautions. If houses are placed in situations where houses ought not to be, or if ill-supplied with drains, water, and proper means of ventilation, an extraordinary amount of ill-health and death results, with as much certainty as that heat comes from fire. Continuing our exposition of the condition of parts of London, let us add a few notes of places through which we have walked recently. Take, for example, Gilbert-street, near the Bear-yard, Lincoln's-inn-fields. "Here," says an informant (pointing to the places), "are about six slaughter-houses within a few yards; a large tripe-boiler's - the effluvium from which is very bad; - stables for horses, &c. You may stand and throw a stone from one of these slaughter-houses to another. Look into this one house [we refrain from giving the number]; you see the water is coming in; there is one cask capable of holding about fifty gallons, another a little more. There is no tap in these casks, so each person is obliged to dip vessels, however dirty, into the water. This supply is for three small houses, containing five families of from five to six persons each: this number the people allow, but some of them being Irish, it is probable that they have lodgers. The people do not like to drink the water from the casks. If they can catch a little when it is coming in they take it home; if not, they go to the spring of Lincoln's-inn."

This dwelling-place has two slaughter-houses at the back, a closet close to the water, a dust-heap, and an open gully-hole in front. The smell of this place is shocking. A respectable shop-keeper opposite has never had her health since she came in the neighbourhood. In her house the water is in the cellar. Standing in this place a person pointed out a house in which two children had been ill of fever, and where one was ill of some complaint at the time. At the corner a young woman is dying, and they blame the bad air. In a house on the opposite side of the street a person is lying dead-close to Bear-yard. We went at random into a house in Sheppard-street, close by. The drain is stopped: the smell, even before passing the threshold, is frightful. Within, we find a clean place, but an atmosphere of a most dangerous nature: we dive into the cellar; here is the closet, the water-cask, and but little ventilation. The effect of such conditions it is fearful to contemplate. So bad was this place, that we were glad to rush out into the somewhat purer air. Any whose duty it is to inquire will receive a sad account from the people living here and round about. All the neighbourhood is in a bad state-a state dangerous under favourable circumstances, but fearful if we consider the condition and poverty of many of the inhabitants. Take one specimen-namely, the occupant of the house in which the children have been ill. The woman, who was washing, was pale and careworn, the room with its little furniture squalid and dirty; a sick child was in the cradle, over which she had watched for death several nights. She had scarcely had any food, "things are getting so dear," she said, "for such people as us. I could not wash yesterday, I had neither fire nor soap. People don't know how hard poverty is: I took that poor child's clothes and pawned them for 4d. here is the ticket: I was advised to get Port wine for the child, I got twopenny worth, there it is nearly all of it left [showing us a small bottle], the poor thing cannot take it. I bought bread with the other 2d. My other children have been ill; I have got an admission for them into the hospital. I pay 3s. a week rent for this place, but owe several weeks. The landlord, who is kind, is getting very impatient."

It must be a hard heart that can hear such a story as this unmoved. But we are not dealing with poverty or the causes of distress; and we have no great admiration for that charity which makes beggars : but these are times and circumstances when those who have means should put aside their political economy, and think merely how to lessen the misery before them. Our more legitimate object and real purpose in mentioning such cases is to show that we have poverty of the intensest kind placed under the worst circumstances, and so to make evident the need of permanent improvements.

The supply of pure water to the poor in their own dwellings on *Sundays* and other days is a matter of paramount necessity; they should not be obliged to "hunt about and " beg for water. Let us hear what the people say in another quarter, namely, Middle Serle's-place."

"The people are forced to run about and beg for water; that they do; I have to do so myself, so I know. Very often the people do their cleaning on the Saturday night: it is now twenty minutes past five, and by half-past seven this evening we shall not have a drop of water." The south side of Serle's-place, which contains many houses, thickly inhabited, is "dry," as the people express it, on Sundays. On the opposite side of the way, the people are better off, the landlord having provided large and substantial water-tanks above ground, properly covered.

In the neighbourhood of Serle's-place, Clement's-lane, and the little alleys running in various directions, the filth is very great, and here fever is a constant visitor. In one court, occupied by a dealer in fancy dogs, and some other persons, there were two untrapped gully-holes; the people had complained in vain to the landlady to have these holes examined, as they were nearly poisoned, and the landlady supplied them with two pieces of wood, imagining that this would be sufficient to stop the escape of the poisonous gases. In the house of the dog-dealer, some time since, the drain became stopped; a young man, the son of the occupant, at that time in perfect health, opened the drain, and in a few days he died of a raging fever! The death of the son killed the father.

With reference to water, we must return once more to Agar-town. No words would be too strong to describe the miserable condition of this disgraceful location. Fever has been raging here, and, as the medical attendant of the district says, " What is the use of giving medicine - when such a condition of things exists?"

Fig. 15. - *The Water coming in at Agar-town.*

Look at Cambridge-terrace. All the refuse water here remains at times on the surface, for the small pipe-drains are constantly being choked. There are open cesspools here. After a heavy shower of rain, the water floods the houses, there being no sufficient channels to convey it away. The whole of the surface of the ground is impregnated with impure matter. In the winter-time, the roadways are a mass of soft mud. At the time of our last visit, pools of stagnant water were collected here, and some black as ink, having on the surface a ghastly bloom, something like the effect produced by the mixture of coal-tar with water. This water passes below the houses of the people, where it remains from year's end to year's end.

Fig. 16.

Here is Victoria Cottage, with the black, poisonous stream passing through the garden, and below the boarding of the house. In this and the houses adjoining the people took up parts of their floors to show us the accumulation of filthy fluid below the beds of themselves and their children.

In another part of this neighbourhood, shown in the engraving, the people were anxious we should see it between four and five o'clock in the afternoon, when the water comes m. As soon as the small water-casks belonging to the houses round about became full, the overflow passed into the court and places adjoining; the water collected to a considerable depth, flowing into several of the houses, and the people were obliged to pass from place to place on stepping-stones; one man said that he had two feet of water in and below his room, and that snails, spiders, and other vermin were plentiful, "crawling over his clothes at night."

"It is a dreadful task," writes one to us, "a task to make the heart ache and the head fail-to revolve in powerless silence the manifold misery of the London poor. Imagination dare not dwell alone upon the probable ravages of death among wretches huddled upon a few rotten planks over reeking cesspools, inhaling the breath that streams from the huge nostrils of drafty sewers, or chained to the gates of men who poison their fellow creatures in scoffing security. As pestilence, ere it strikes home, tears aside the veil, we behold, once more and perforce, what we dare to call the 'daily life' of thousands of our countrymen. Who must account for the lives of those innocent multitudes that you fling from the very cradle into the grave; or of those, more horribly, that you refuse to slay till you have made the soul brutal and hideous as the carcass that holds it? Do we not know that if the armies of England were placed in such deadly peril as are at this moment some 200,000 of the inhabitants of this metropolis,-nay, if it were a question of 200 refugees, - they would be rescued, though it cost us, as the *Times* would say, 'the last ounce of our treasure, and the last drop of our blood?' Can we affirm that in the present instance there will be expended as much intellect, as much activity, as much gold as went to compass 500 seats at a general election? Vain is it for you, at life's peril, to seize the images of these infernal horrors, and drag them into the upper day; for, amongst all those wonderful forms in which Anglo-Saxon wisdom has wrapped its laws, none can be found to stay a plague. For the stealing of twopenny-worth of cheese there is punishment prompt enough to slay one's tenants, to poison one's neighbours, are safe and easy crimes, the stain of which may be washed from one's name with ever so little Cologne water. Your baths and washhouses, your schools of industry and art, are good things, and well enough to a man who can go home to a few cubic yards of respirable air, a few cubic yards of dry soil, who has a few feet of pipe to bring him water, a few more to carry away his refuse out of sight and smell, who finds a place there which he can enter without dismay, and leave without despair. But what need he care for them in his present misery? A man must have heroic courage and constancy, who can adorn such places as you have shown us with the virtues of sobriety, cleanliness, and *thought.*"

In 1849, statistical details, partially ascertained, induced the suspicion that impure water was one of the main sources of the choleraic virus, and it was resolved that should we unhappily be visited with the scourge again, this suspicion should be either verified or disproved by further investigation. In consequence, we find, in a supplement to a recent report from the Registrar-General for the Metropolitan Districts, some important statistics, which go far to show that there *is* a decided connection between the source of water supply and the prevalence of cholera. The subject, however, it must be noted, is mixed up with the ascertained connection of lowness of elevation of site generally with liability to cholera, but even this may resolve itself - we had almost said *must* resolve itself - into the twofold source of probable virus, in impregnation both of air and water. The very poison which pervades the water, in all probability also pervades the air; and, according to the density of that virus, the lower the site the more fully impregnated will both the air and the *water supplied from the same level* be; for as respects water, it is clear, for instance, that the lower the Thames water falls, the impurer it becomes; that water falling from any elevated water-shed must be purer the higher its level; and as respects air, if the cholera virus consist in such impurities from decomposing organic matter as those also contained in water, it will clearly, in the first place, be through the lower stratum of the air resting on the earth, that such impurities as decomposing vegetable and animal matter will be absorbed.

That cholera actually prevails more in low atmospheric levels than in high, as well as more in districts supplied with water from lower than from higher sources, appears from a table lately published in the supplemental report referred to.

It is believed that through almost the whole of this table the impurity of the waters with which the inhabitants of the several districts are supplied, is in nearly a direct proportion to the mortality from cholera.

A most important point in connection with the homes of the poor is involved here. Captain Nelson, of the Engineers, writing to us on the subject, says:-

"A near connection of mine in Wiltshire, not long since built two batches of cottages - one on the upper part of a hill, the other halfway down-both connected by the same line of sewage. The upper batch remained quite healthy, whilst the lower became suddenly the prey of typhus of a malignant type. Both sets of cottages were on the slope of the Great Northern escarpment of the Chalk Downs-the country open, and remarkably healthy; so that my brother-in-law felt much puzzled to account for the mischief: he persevered, however, in his study of the subject, and it occurred to him at last, that although not built many years, it was possible that the sewage might be more or less choked. On investigation, he found that the water of the well of the lower cottages became at times turbid, evidently by matters that found their way through the brick lining of the said well, which was placed *too near* the drain: this last was immediately opened, and the proprietor's suspicion verified. When the drain was put to rights, the disease soon disappeared."

How much longer shall we allow 15,000 persons to be annually cut off, unnaturally and prematurely, in this gay and wealthy metropolis? How much longer shall the pain, misery, and waste of money, consequent on the want of proper sanitary arrangements, be borne and suffered? "Let it be remembered that a sickly population is one of the most costly burdens of a state. Health is the poor man's capital in trade; and whatever deteriorates that entails a direct loss, and eventually a heavy money charge, upon the community. The enormous amount of poverty and destitution in this country, and the consequent necessity for an impost of nearly £8,000,000 sterling annually for its relief, are in a great measure due to the pauperizing effects of preventible disease." But these are not the only social evils involved in this important inquiry. The localities that are the nurseries of sickness and death, are almost invariably found to be the haunts of immorality and crime. Filth and squalor are as productive of moral debasement as of physical depravation; the two natures of man are so intimately connected, that the defilement of the one is generally associated with pollution of the other.

If those who admit the truth of what is constantly being said on this subject, would carry their belief into effect in the course of their practical operations, they would most materially assist in benefiting the world. Routine so thoroughly possesses us, that nine men out of ten who rise from the perusal of an essay showing the evils of some ordinary mode of construction, or of the want of certain arrangements, thoroughly convinced of the truth of it, will, in the next house they build, follow the old road, and continue the erroneous mode, or omit the required arrangements.

From an analysis of 60,000 deaths from consumption which annually take place in England and Wales, the conclusion has been arrived at that tradesmen are nearly twice as liable to consumption as the gentry, "owing chiefly to the hot, close, ill-ventilated workshops, in which the former pass so many hours of the day; that in-door labourers are more subject to consumption than those who follow their employments out of doors, exposed to all the inclemencies of the weather, and earning less wages, and having, consequently, worse food, clothing, and lodging: and that of in-door labourers, those engaged in workshops are more subject to consumption than those employed at home."

What precautionary measures will do for health may be illustrated by reference to the small-pox. In Russia, previous to the introduction of vaccination, one-seventh of the population died of the small-pox. In Denmark, through strict laws relating to vaccination, mortality from small-pox has been scarcely known since 1800. In Bavaria, as long ago as 1820, this disease was exterminated. Yet in England, through care for the liberty of the subject (?), during the three years ending 1840, the average annual number of deaths from small-pox was *twelve thousand!*

It is proved that the money-loss through typhus-fever alone in the metropolis, during the five years 1843-47 was £1,328,000, and that this might have been prevented!

The daily removal of house refuse is of the greatest consequence thousands are slain by its non-removal. When rain falls on a surface loaded with decomposing organic matter (the back-yards of innumerable houses), and it is warmed by the sun, it readily yields to the atmosphere vapours charged with disease and death. We always come back to the fact that the condition of the dwellings of the poor and of the industrial classes is a chief cause of the excess of deaths and of the prevalence of disease, poverty, immorality, and crime.

The physical circumstances in and around a dwelling are a measure of the health and comfort of the tenants. Where there is manifest unfitness for healthy existence, there can be no home-no permanent happiness-no self-respect, or moral elevation of character. Disease *must* come, and with it a whole train of depressing, vitiating, and paupensing influences.

We happened a few weeks ago to be in one of the Thames omnibuses, which flit about on the river from pier to pier like gnats in the sunshine, and had fallen into a reverie on the miserable condition of our noble river, both in bed and on banks. The resident topographer, in the shape of a small boy in very greasy trowsers, recalled us by shouting " Lambeth; Lam-beth." So we stepped ashore, as much to escape the fearful odour which was floating over the water from the mouths of the sewers opened by the retiring tide, as to see what was going on in that neglected and ill-used locality. It is a place full of interest and full of wants; but little endeavour seems to be made to maintain the one or to supply the other.

In the earliest record extant, says Lysons, "it is called Lambehith; in Doomsday Book, probably by mistake, Lanchei; by the ancient historians it is spelt Lamhee, Lamheth, Lambyth, Lamedk." Some etymologists derive the name from *Lam*, dirt, and *hyd* or *hythe*, a haven; others from Lamb and hythe. For our own part we incline greatly to the "dirt" derivation, and would appeal to the present state of much of the district in confirmation of the opinion. Many obvious improvements suggest themselves, and there are some earnest men, dwellers there, who would assist : still nothing is done. Parts of the parish, lying near the river, are often under water; the drainage is very bad, and the general condition of the district discreditable to our age and knowledge. The bone-manure works and other factories contaminate the air; and the water with which the inhabitants are supplied was, until very recently, if it is not now, taken from the river in dangerous proximity to the mouth of the common sewer. In the first report of the Metropolitan Sanitary Commission, evidence was given that in some of the courts and streets fever was always present. At that time the average duration of life there was *twenty-four* years, while at Camberwell it was thirty-four!

There are some miserable dog-holes of dwellings in Lambeth, although not worse than in many other districts, - murderous houses, - death-dealers, which no efforts on the part of the occupants will render healthful or decent.

In a pamphlet on "Home Reform," by Mr. Roberts, published by the Society for Improving the Condition of the Labouring Classes, with the laudable object of answering some who, in reference to the same writer's "Essay on the Dwellings of the Labouring Classes," have asked, how their tenants might be taught to improve their own homes, - the writer says:-

"We must begin by insisting that, however much of the physical and moral evils of the working classes may be justly attributable to their dwellings, it is too often the case that more ought in truth to be imputed to themselves. For surely the inmate depends less on the house, than the house on the inmate; mind has more power over matter than matter over mind. Let a dwelling be ever so poor and incommodious, yet a family with decent and cleanly habits will contrive to make the best of it, and will take care that there shall be nothing offensive in it which they have power to remove. Whereas a model house, fitted up with every convenience and comfort which modern science can supply, will, if occupied by persons of intemperate and uncleanly habits, speedily become a disgrace and a nuisance. A sober, industrious, and cleanly couple will impart an air of decency and respectability to the poorest dwelling; while the spendthrift, the drunkard, or the gambler, will convert a palace into a scene of discomfort and disgust. Since, therefore, so much depends on the character and conduct of the parties themselves, it is right that they should feel their responsibility in this important matter, and that they should know and attend to the various points connected with the improvement of their homes.

This is, to a certain extent, true, and it is of the utmost importance that it should be constantly and widely impressed. It must not, however, be taken as an excuse for not providing innoxious, decent, and comely dwellings for the working classes. Much may be done by an energetic orderly mind in any situation; but there are hundreds and hundreds of dwellings that ultimately beat every occupier, and transform the tidy housewife into the slatternly shrew, and the industrious home-loving husband into a disorderly drunkard. Where there is no "mind," "matter" has it all on its own way, of course; and how is it possible that an orderly mind,-careful of proprieties, anxious to improve, sensitive against evil,-can be manufactured, or even maintained, amidst darkness, dampness, disorder, and discomfort. As we have often heard clergymen say, sermons, exhortations, visitings, and the national school, are all useless against a damp, dilapidated, ill-drained, miserable dwelling, where decency is not possible, and immorality inevitable.

> Occasionally you may find some who have
> "The equal temper of heroic hearts
> Made weak by time and fate, but strong in will
> To strive, to seek, to find, *and not to yield.*"

But these are rare exceptions.

The moral and physical effects of the present condition of things, the great degradation, ill-health, and loss of life, meet us at every turn. Typhus, the disease of filth, has been busy. Those who have been engaged in the relief of some of the London parishes, tell a sad tale of the great expense and loss of life constantly resulting from dirt, ill-drainage, and bad air. Not long since a man called on one so engaged, and asked to be assisted with a coffin in which to bury his wife, being too poor to provide one, in consequence of her sudden death from typhus fever. After two or three hours he came back for another coffin: one of his children had died. In the course of the same day he came back for two more: in all, four had died: in less than two days he was carried off himself. On another occasion, our informant was sent for to visit a house, and found three dead bodies on the floor, no bed in the room, and the place filled with people. Thus fever sweeps the ill-conditioned neighbourhoods. A remedy must be found-the mere pulling down of dilapidated and disreputable buildings is of no avail-it is only removing the poor from one district to another, and is no doubt at the present time raising the cost of rent to those who have the least means of paying it.

We once overheard a conversation between a veteran compositor and a young author: the latter was insisting that a certain amount of matter should be put into a particular space. "Type, sir," said the printer, "is not india-rubber, which can be pressed into less than its natural bulk." Human beings, like the compositor's type, also require a certain amount of space. The number of poor - the very poor - is unfortunately great in London, and this class must be provided for. In all directions the dwellings of the worst sort are being swept away: within the last few years, hundreds of houses have been demolished in the City liberties, in Marylebone, St. Clement's Danes, and other parishes too numerous - to mention. Persons congratulate themselves on the removal of "rookeries," and look with complacency at the noble warehouses and streets which rise to occupy the sites of the wretched hovels. But what has been done in this great metropolis to provide for the living creatures who, by the improvements, have had their hearths destroyed? Literally nothing. A short time ago we witnessed the ejectment, from Orchard-place, Portman-square, of nearly 1,500 men, women, and children: the place was in a bad condition, and fever was a constant visitor; yet the people were sorry to~ leave the place, knowing the difficulty of obtaining, with their limited means, a better lodging, or even any lodging at all. Single men could manage well enough, but it was distressing to see the wretched furniture, if so it could be called, and families in the muddy street on a rainy day, the parents hunting in all directions to obtain shelter. These poor people would go, as a matter of course, to the already thickly-crowded parts of Marylebone, St. Pancras, Clerkenwell, &c., for no provision had been made for them of an improved kind. "We must try our relations, for my husband cannot get a lodging," said a woman sitting in the rain, with her children, and some household goods which would not be to a broker worth half-a-crown; "surely they must take in their own flesh and blood." Poor things!

The Associations for improving the dwellings of the industrious classes in London, have not yet extended their aid to the large class to which we are alluding; they have, however, done much to remove the prejudice against new and convenient dwellings: respectable mechanics and others have gladly availed themselves of the private and convenient arrangements of the so-called "model houses," which where placed in eligible situations, will be a certain source of profit to their constructors.

This condition of things is a sad fact, which not only distresses the poor population of London, but other large cities. Many have no doubt sunk by misfortune and their own faults into these "immortal sewers," as the Rev. G. S. Osborne has called the dark shadows of city life; and thousands are born here and placed in circumstances where the chance of leading a proper life is almost hopeless. Education is but of little use to those living in filthy lanes and such over-crowded dwellings as have come under our observation. The first great means of raising the poorest classes is to reform their dwellings, to provide places wholesome and well ordered, at rents which they can afford to pay. We want, in London, first, decent yet not luxurious sleeping accommodation and means of washing, &c., for those who are entirely destitute; secondly, rooms for poor families, in which the members of them can be kept distinct, at rents ranging from 1s. 6d. to 2s. and 2s. 6d. a week. We believe that dwellings of this description, extensively carried out in a proper method and well constructed, would be attended with great benefit, and, moreover, would pay: and thirdly, the erection of houses in flats, at rents of from 4s. to 10s. per week, the extent and finish to be according to the rent.

We have asserted that disease can be lessened by sanitary arrangements. The evidence to this effect is undeniable, and it has been largely increased by Dr. Southwood Smith's pamphlet, before alluded to.

The writer shows, first, that the buildings for families erected by the societies afforded a return last year of nearly 5 per cent. on the outlay; secondly, that while the deaths in the whole metropolis during the year 1852 reached the proportion of 22 and a fraction in the thousand (that is, 22 persons died in every 1,000), the mortality in the establishments of the association (the average of the whole) was but 7 and a fraction; "consequently, the total mortality in London generally, taking together all classes, rich and poor, was proportionally more than three times greater than the mortality in these establishments." In the Kensington Potteries, the deaths equalled 40 in 1,000!

We *know* that it is necessary to eat to maintain life, and we eat; we *know* that if the hand be put into the fire, it will be burnt, and we take care not to put it there; we equally well know that by the provision of salubrious dwellings for the labouring chasses, - fresh air, pure water, and good drainage, - we save money, suffering, virtue, and life; and in the name of all we hold in reverence, let us endeavour to provide them!

It is impossible to over-estimate the practical importance of the results which are now before the world,- "They show," says Dr. Smith, "the extent to which, under circumstances of the utmost difficulty and danger, it may still be possible to save life: they open a prospect of the physical and social improvement of the people, such as, before these results were obtained, there was no warrant from experience to anticipate : they indicate that the first step in this progress must be the removal of the degrading influence of the present dwellings of the labouring classes, and they prove the practicability, without loss to the capitalist, or additional rent to the tenant, of the universal substitution of houses for hovels. There must be compulsory enforcement of certain sanitary conditions wherever there are human habitations. There must be provision for the supply of better-ordered dwellings for the industrious classes: dwellings accessible to air and light, and no longer producing that malarious depression which resorts for relief to the fatal stimulus of ardent spirits: dwellings compatible with cleanliness, comfort, and those decent observances which are necessary to self-respect, and which must become habits before there can be respect for the happiness, property, or life of others. Until such dwellings are within the reach of these classes, they cannot be raised out of that physical debasement which has lately been so painfully depicted, and which has been shown to be the portion (the unnecessary portion) of large masses of the people. The physical improvement of these masses, it is now admitted, must precede their intellectual and moral elevation. When the house ceases to be a sty, and possesses the conditions which render it capable of being made a home, then, but not till then, may it receive, with some hope of benefit, the schoolmaster and the minister of religion."

CHAPTER XI.

HIGH-STREET, Southwark-High-street in the Borough, as the Londoners call it-presents a busy scene on a Saturday night - probably every night, - but it was Saturday night when we last saw it. A countless throng streams along the pavement, omnibuses and carts fill the wide roadway, and the shops are blazing with light. Lightest of all these and most numerous are the linen-drapers' and grocers', before which the crowd oftenest breaks at one of the latter it stands still, so that those who would pass on must go into the road. It stands still that it may read the "poetry" in the window, wherein the generous proprietor, most anxious to serve his fellow creatures, actually says,-

However wonderful, however strange,
We take old coin and give new in exchange-
That is, if you will buy our coffee, so good,
Which has long been the best in the neighbourhood."

An ingenious offer of - nothing, grandiloquently. Where all the people are going, and how they all live, are subjects for speculation; but there they are, and, as we just now said, it is a bright and busy scene.

Here and there women and children are sitting at what would seem to be extra doors to some of the houses, but if you penetrate the darkness you will find these are the mouths of courts, to which they have come to see the world, and get some fresher air, and you begin to have an idea of what may he behind all the brightness and bustle. Nor in walking here can you quite confine your thoughts to the Present you remember, as you pass one house, that Chaucer wrote-

"Befell that in that season, on a day,
In Southwarke, at the *Tabard,* as I lay,
Readie to wander on my Pilgrimage
To Canterburie with devout courage," -

Came there the "nine-and-twentie in a companie," whose persons, minds, and adventures he has placed so vividly and enduringly before us, that we have a much better knowledge of them than we have of the majority of our own living acquaintances.

Southwark (Suthgeweorke, as it was called as early as 1023), is springled with interesting associations, recalled here and there even by the names of the streets. In early times it had a bad character: in 1327, when it had come into the hands of the Crown by some means, the citizens of London showed King Edward III. that felons and thieves, privily departing from the City into Southwark, where they could not be attached by the officers of the City, were openly received and harboured there; and the king, in accordance with their prayer, granted the town of Southwark to the Corporation of London for ever. This, the old town, however, was but a small portion of what we know as the Borough, and is what is now called the Guildable Manor, extending from St. Mary Overy's Dock westward, to Hay's-lane, Tooley-street, by the side of Hay's Wharf eastward, running west along Tooley-street a certain distance, then going south to the High-street as far as the Town-hall, and at the back of the Town-hall to Counter-street, and thence to St. Mary Overy's Dock. The other Manors, viz, the King's Manor and the Great Liberty Manor, were not part of the Borough until they were purchased by the Corporation of London from King Edward VI.

The turning at the south end of High-street, opposite St. George's Church, is Mint-street.* [* St. George's Church was designed by John Price, architect. The first stone was laid on the 23rd of April, 1734. In the old church here the arithmetician Cocker, "according to whom people so often speak, was buried.] Here stood Suffolk-place, a noble mansion, erected by Charles Brandon, duke of Suffolk. A view of it is given in a drawing by Anthony Van Den Wyngrerde, made about 1546, and engraved in Mr. Brayley's excellent "History of Surrey." The duke gave this house to Henry VIII. who was his brother-in-law, in exchange for a palace in St. Martin's-in-the-Fields, and in it the king established a mint for coinage. We may say, by the way, that there was a mint in Southwark in earlier times, but this was without doubt in the old town, the Guildable Manor.* [* Mr. G. R. Corner, who has well investigated the antiquities of the Borough, thinks that the ancient Mint was most likely at the place commonly described as the Prior of Lewes's Hostelry, but which he considers was the house of a frater. nity, brotherhood, or guild of Jesus; the guildhall, probably, of the ancient town of Southwark. It came into the hands of the parish of St. Olave by grant from the Brethren of Jesus, with licence from King Henry VIII. confirmed by Edward VI. and became the Vestry-hall of the parish.]

After vicissitudes, Suffolk-place, or "the Mint," was sold : a great part of it was pulled down, and on its site many small cottages were built, as Stowe says, "to the increasing of beggars in the Borough." The district became the resort of lawless persons, the privilege of exemption from legal process being claimed for it : it was an Alsatia, a sanctuary for evil nor was any proper control obtained there until 1723. Here died Nahum Tate, once poet laureate: and Pope constantly refers to the place as a residence of poor poets in his writings. *Mat o' the Mint,* it will be remembered, is a character in the "Beggars' Opera."

But we must get back from the past to what more immediately concerns us; so let us walk up this Mint-street out of the busy thoroughfare described at starting. Its evil character has not departed from it. With a gin-shop at the High-street end, and St. George's Workhouse at the other, it has on either side of it con genes of filthy courts unfit for habitation. The houses are tumbling down, the approaches in a miserable condition, as may be seen in Fig. 17. Let us take one of the courts on the south side of it - Wallis's-alley, where the houses (of wood) are in the most distressing state of dilapidation : the ceilings have fallen, the floors are full of holes, and the windows glassless. "I have but two panes," said a poor old woman, living in the upper part of one of them, "in my two rooms." In this house, for which the landlord receives 2s. per week for the front room on the ground floor; 1s. 6d. for the back room; 1s. 6d. for the front room above, and 1s. 3d. for two small back rooms on that floor,-equal to £16. 5s. per annum, there are fifteen persons living, and we may consider that there are at least the same number in each of the adjoining three tenements. For the "convenience" of this body of people there is a hole in the rotting back-yard, but partly covered by two or three planks and a dilapidated seat there is no door, no enclosure, other than a few boards, three or four feet high from the ground The decomposing contents of the open cesspool beneath contaminate the air around, and decency is out of the question.

We can scarcely restrain ourselves to speak calmly on such abominations.

A short time ago two men opened a cesspool in Pelham-street, Spitalfields, and, becoming suddenly exposed to its foul gas, both died! In the case of those who die more slowly, the cause is not recognised.

To the blind persistence in the answer to inquirers, given by the occupants of such places as the Mint, that they enjoy very good health, and that their place is very wholesome, we have again and again referred; but it cannot be too often spoken of for the guidance of those engaged in sanitary investigations. In the immediate neighbourhood of the court just now mentioned, we asked two women as to their health, and received the usual answer. Will it be believed that, on farther questioning, we found the first had had seven children, but that only one was alive, and that the second bad been the mother of thirteen, *and that the whole were dead?* This is no invention : we assert it solemnly as a dreadful fact.

In Wallis's-alley there is a tap at one end, where the water runs for about a quarter of an hour each morning, and the inhabitants have to catch what they can. On Sundays they have none. The approach is unpaved; the general condition a disgrace to the locality. Visiting the neighbourhood again, in the daylight, we found in the courts adjoining, "conveniences without doors, and rotting dung-heaps on all sides. In Mitre-court, the general dust-bin had not been emptied for more than three weeks, according to the statement of the in-habitants. Here the water does not run until night, sometimes as late as eleven o'clock "When we are forced, said a woman, "to wait for one another, it runs so slowly; and some of us have nothing to store it in when it does come. "On Sundays, said another, "I and my children are miserably off: it is no use trying to be clean. In South Sea-court, running into Southwark-bridge-road, the refuse lies rotting on the unpaved road. Though boasting such names as King-street, Queen-street, Duke-street, the whole district has an aspect of poverty and misery; and we were not surprised, though a little startled at the moment, to find a sufferer from cholera in one of the rooms we entered.

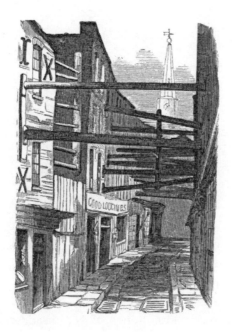

Fig. 17 - Mint-street, looking towards High-street.

Fig. 18 - Duke-street. Southwark

Fig. 19 - At the back of Ewer-street, Gravel-lane

As the poverty and distress, so would seem to be the number of children. In one of the courts, on entering, we counted thirty-seven children at play: merry little things, as yet unsaddened or debased; pure little souls, ready to take any impress!

A few years ago some influential inhabitants of the Borongh sought to improve this neighbourhood by forming a new street from Blackman-street, where it joins High-street, to Southwark-bridge-road, and farther, and an Act of Parliament for it was obtained. Funds, however, could not be raised; the scheme was abandoned, and the place remains in the sad condition of which we have given but a faint notion. Inquiries were being made, we understood, by a committee of the inhabitants of the parish with a view to some ameliorations; what resulted we know not.

As a matter of course, some will think that the Borough "Mint " cannot surely be so bad as we have described it to be. So far from having exaggerated, our feeble words give but a weak idea of the miserable condition of this neighbourhood. Fig. 18 is a sketch of Duke-street, where it adjoins Queen-street. Fig. 19 represents a location called James's-place, behind Ewer-street. The latter is a long street of dilapidated houses, partly wood, which comes into Gravel-lane. The drainage is here most defective; and according to an old inhabitant,- In this and the surrounding neighbourhood were formerly many open ditches, into which the tide regularly ebbed and flowed; these have been covered, and now form 'blind drains.' Even now the tides often overflow parts of this street to a depth of from 2 to 3 feet. The cellars about here are often flooded. The houses are dilapidated, and as a matter of course, have cesspools at the back, many of them without even a covering. The health of the people is very bad: fever, we were told, had killed many lately in Ewer-street, and the courts leading from it. In Red Lion-court, a neighbour said "there have been lately several deaths." Here are cesspools and choked surface drains, which at the time of our visit were undergoing inspection. The place at the back of Ewer-street, which we have sketched, contains twenty or thirty houses. It would be difficult, either by words or illustrations, to give an idea of the squalid and unhealthy condition of this spot. The houses are unfit for occupation: at the back is a large dust-heap. If this disgraceful and unwholesome accumulation be disposed of at the present time, it may be at a loss to the proprietor ; but surely this is not to be set against the lives of men, women, and children? The pavement of this neglected place is broken and uneven, strewed with refuse amid puddles of -water. Sometimes, in parts, the water is up to the knees of the people. The houses are thickly inhabited chiefly by Irish: there are only four closets, with cesspools, for the use of the neighbourhood, and these -we found in a dreadful condition.

If the thousands who are still streaming past the blazing shops in the High-street, were made to understand and feel thoroughly the loss produced to *themselves* in money, health, safety, and life, by the close, unpaved, ill-drained, vitiated, and vitiating dens behind, we should soon have matters put in train to bring about a better state of things not only in the "Borough Mint," but in the other places we have described.

Reader! we have not written for your amusement, but for your knowledge and consideration. Accept the endeavour for the sake of the motive.

Lightning Source UK Ltd.
Milton Keynes UK
06 July 2010

156620UK00002B/1/P